THE
Labrador
HANDBOOK

Your Definitive Guide to Care and Training

Pippa Mattinson

EBURY
PRESS

13 5 7 9 10 8 6 4 2

Ebury Press, an imprint of Ebury Publishing, 20 Vauxhall Bridge Road, London SW1V 2SA

Ebury Press is part of the Penguin Random House group of companies whose addresses can be found at global.penguinrandomhouse.com

Penguin
Random House
UK

Text copyright © Pippa Mattinson 2015

Picture credits:

Heidrun Humphries: 2, 8, 25, 32, 84, 87, 91, 169; Jon Lane: 6; Nick Ridley: 14, 36, 37, 41, 44, 52, 56, 60, 62, 71, 89, 96, 110, 118, 132, 141, 147, 148, 151, 171, 173, 178, 179, 185; Pippa Mattinson: 18, 28, 38, 66, 79, 139, 145, 154; Rhian White www.brightondogphotography.co.uk: 7, 16, 21, 22, 26, 30, 75, 77, 101, 106, 120, 123, 124, 129, 137, 176

First published by Ebury Press in 2015

www.eburypublishing.co.uk

A CIP catalogue record for this book is available from the British Library

ISBN 9781785030918

Printed and bound in China by C&C Offset printing co.,Ltd

MIX
Paper from
responsible sources
FSC® C018179

Penguin Random House is committed to a sustainable future for our business, our readers and our planet. This book is made from Forest Stewardship Council® certified paper.

Contents

Pippa Mattinson is a zoologist and the founder of The Gundog Trust – the UK's first gundog training and welfare charity. She is a keen supporter of modern, science-based dog training methods, and is passionate about helping people to enjoy their dogs. Visit her website for more information: www.pippamattinson.com

Introduction

The Labrador Retriever is surely one of the most loved and respected pedigree dog breeds in the world. In the United Kingdom, and in the USA, it is certainly the most numerous. There are over two hundred different breeds of dog to choose from in Britain, yet in 2014, around 16 per cent of all the pedigree puppies registered with the Kennel Club, were Labradors. That's one in every six puppies. No other breed comes close.

While a well-trained adult Labrador is the ultimate human companion, getting to the well-trained and adult part can be difficult at times. Young Labradors can be boisterous and destructive, and they need consistent guidance and handling in order to fulfil their potential. In 2011, I set up a website, the Labrador Site, to help people overcome some of the challenges involved in raising a Labrador puppy, training their companion and coping with owning a large, bouncy dog. Over twelve thousand visitors currently browse the hundreds of articles in the Labrador Site archives each day, and one of the objectives of this book is to bring together the wealth of information accumulated on the site, so that you can have it on your bedside table, to read and refer to at your leisure.

This book is very much my personal approach to a breed of dog that I have shared my life with for over thirty years. I won't be giving you long lists of Labrador diseases, labelled diagrams of the workings of your Labrador's reproductive organs, or lengthy descriptions of breed history or characteristics. These are covered adequately elsewhere. My aim is to take you on a journey through the life of the Labrador from puppyhood to old age, pausing here and there to cover specific age-related issues in more detail. I want to help you with the common problems that thousands of people have posted up on our website, so that you and your dog can resolve them quickly or even avoid them altogether.

With the right support and encouragement, raising a Labrador should be fun for your entire family. With that in mind, almost everything in this book is aimed at dealing with the realities of raising and training a large, intelligent and powerful dog so that he is a credit to you and a joy to all who know him. We'll be examining some of the challenges that will face us along the way, from the perils of potty training, through the agonies of adolescence, to the relative calm of maturity and onwards to the twilight years, addressing all the decisions and responsibilities that each stage brings.

I'll be showing you how to use the best and most up-to-date training methods, and including exercises that help build your skill and develop your dog's potential as well as providing entertainment and amusement for you both. Since a book can only do so much, I'll also be showing you how and where to find help if you get stuck at any point.

Raising a Labrador is one of life's very best experiences. Like every adventure, there will be challenges and surprises, but with a little help and support this will be a journey that you will thoroughly enjoy.

1

A special friendship

For many of us, the Labrador has come to represent the perfect canine partner. No other breed of dog inspires such admiration and devotion in so many human beings, and no other breed of dog has come to serve our needs in such a multitude of roles. The characteristics of this ordinary yet very extraordinary dog are so widely recognised and accepted that even those who have never owned a Labrador are able to describe his personality and are happy to acknowledge his value to society.

It is fascinating to consider what makes the Labrador so special and admired. He is not without his flaws, and can be challenging to manage in his boisterous adolescence. So why do we love this bouncy, messy, food-obsessed creature with such a passion? Could the clue to the success of the world's most popular dog lie somewhere in his past?

The St John's dog

The origins of the Labrador as a unique breed are well known and documented. The history of the Labrador goes back over two hundred years, when our modern dogs' ancestors were living and working in Newfoundland. Today's Labrador Retriever is descended from the St John's dog of North America. These fishermen's assistants, probably descended from the larger Newfoundland dogs, were noted for their love of water and of retrieving, and for their excellent temperament. As a result, they soon became popular hunting and sporting dogs, too. The first St John's dogs were imported into England in the early 1800s, and it was in Britain that the breed as we know it today was established.

The first Labradors

St John's dogs were established in the United Kingdom by two British aristocrats, independently of each other, both of whom were impressed by the retrieving abilities of these adaptable and hardy dogs. The name Labrador was used early on and probably came about due to the location of Labrador in the region from which the dogs were imported. The first breeding kennel was established by the 2nd Earl of Malmesbury in the early1800s and, a few years later, another was set up by the 5th Duke of Buccleuch.

The Buccleuch breeding programme laid the foundation of the modern working Labrador Retriever we know and love and is still going strong today! The Kennel Club recognised the Labrador Retriever as a pedigree breed in 1903, and the Labrador has become increasingly popular over succeeding generations, as a service dog, family pet and favourite all-round shooting companion. Despite the huge variety of roles played by the Labrador over the years, it is his origins as a retriever that have made him uniquely suited to some of the vital roles he plays in our modern world.

Gundog heritage

The Kennel Club allocates all breeds of dog to one of seven groups. The Gundog Group embraces dogs that have been bred for many years specifically to act as hunting companions. The requirements of this role have influenced some of the characteristics of the gundog breeds, especially in terms of temperament. Some of these breed characteristics persist today, even though the majority of modern gundogs are no longer worked in the shooting field. There are four sub-groups, or categories, of gundog work – the retrievers, the pointers, the spaniels, and the HPRs (hunt, point, retrieve).

The retrievers are expected to find shot game, such as rabbits, duck or pheasant, and return the dead animal to their human partner in a fit state for the table. The spaniels and HPRs are expected to retrieve, too, but retriever breeds are the ultimate specialists at this job. There are other very successful working retriever breeds – most of you will be familiar with the Golden Retriever, and the less numerous Flatcoated Retriever – but the world of the working retriever is dominated by the Labrador. Not only is he the most popular and successful companion dog; he is also the most successful working retriever in history.

Labradors have a strong instinct to pick up and carry objects.

What makes a Labrador?

The Labrador is so familiar that he needs little description. Like all gundogs, every young Labrador is an athlete in the making, with huge capacity for endurance, speed and agility. He covers his ground at an easy gallop and, with his otter tail, dense waterproof coat and the right up-bringing, is as at home in the water as he is on land.

Just as they do for every pedigree dog, the Kennel Club publishes a 'breed standard' for the Labrador Retriever, as a guide to exactly how an adult Labrador should be structured, and what his temperament should be. The Kennel Club describes a kindly, intelligent dog, around 56 centimetres (22 inches) high at the shoulder, and with no trace of aggression – an adaptable and devoted companion. Undoubtedly, these important characteristics are what we expect from the breed and, for the most part, that is what we get.

The Kennel Clubs of the UK and North America recognise just three colours of Labrador – yellow, black and brown. Brown dogs are usually referred to as chocolate, or occasionally by the original term, liver. Yellow dogs may come in a whole range of shades, from pale cream to the deepest fox-red. All these shades must be registered as yellow. Strictly speaking, there is no such thing as a Golden Labrador.

The breed is not without controversy. At some point during the last fifty years, a gene that causes dilution of coat colour has appeared and created a new silver colour, one that most of us will be more familiar with in the Weimaraner breed. Many people find the colour both attractive and appealing, and many others consider it an outrage. Controversy continues over how this gene got into the Labrador breed. It is possible that it appeared via a genetic mutation but perhaps more likely that it arrived via a surreptitious outcross between a Labrador and a Weimaraner. In the absence of any real proof, Kennel Clubs are (probably reluctantly) accepting registrations of dogs with the new colour, although they must be registered by the original colour that has been diluted (black or brown), not under the colour silver.

Controversy over breed appearance is not limited to colour. Over the last few decades, a division in type has arisen within the breed, and not only in structure and appearance, but in temperament, too.

A divided breed

At one time, a Labrador could theoretically win a prize in the show ring one day and win a field trial the next. However, over time, the two types have become deeply divided. It's important to understand the difference between these two strains of Labrador, because the strain you choose to bring into your life may have some bearing on how well you get along together. Although in the USA the dogs on either side of this division are sometimes referred to as English (show type) and American (field type), this is a bit of a misnomer, since the division is exactly the same in the UK. We have show and field Labradors, too, and both are British in origin. The division between the two types is one of purpose, not one of nationality.

Field or working-strain Labradors

Field or working-type Labradors are athletic, lean dogs with less substance than the Labradors of old. Some have lost the classic Labrador otter tail, some have a thinner coat than the modern show Labrador, and in some cases, on the working dog, the handsome chiselled Labrador head has become a little snipey. The working Labrador is often quite sensitive and biddable, and at the same time,

It's important to choose the right type of Labrador for your family.

highly driven and energetic. He is a fast and very powerful animal, surprisingly agile for a relatively large dog, and capable of leaping gates and fences with ease. The working-strain Labrador is very soft mouthed and has a natural ability to mark and find fallen game, and, often, an overpowering urge to retrieve. These attributes, together with his receptive attitude to training, all help to account for his continued success in the shooting field and beyond. Most working-strain Labradors make great companion dogs, but some have such energy and drive that they may be a challenge for the inexperienced pet-dog owner to manage.

Show or bench-strain Labradors

The show-type Labrador has become a more heavyweight and, in some cases, less agile animal than his ancestors and field-bred cousins. Some show Labradors now have rather short legs compared with the Labradors of the twentieth century, and there seems to be no clear explanation for this. There may be some differences in temperament, too. Show-type dogs may, in some cases, be a bit more emotionally robust, playful and devil may care about life, and may lack the intense drive of the field-bred dog, but these are by no means predictable attributes. For example, my younger, mainly show-line Labrador is as keen a retriever as any of my working-line dogs.

Some Labrador enthusiasts feel that show lines have become too heavy and lack the agility and stamina for their original purpose. Despite this concern, and although they may not be successful in top-level competitions, many show-bred Labradors are currently working successfully as retrievers on shoots up and down the country. So, owning a show-type Labrador is not a barrier to participating in gundog fieldwork.

Which type is right for you?

It is always difficult to make sweeping generalisations about which strain of Labrador is right for any particular family. Many families will be very happy with a Labrador from either field or show stock. *Some* field-bred Labradors can prove a challenge outdoors since they have strong hunting instincts, but, for the most part, it is really a matter of personal choice.

As a rough guideline, it's best to choose a dog from working lines if you are interested in sports requiring an athletic and agile dog. Activities such as agility or working trials are best suited to working-strain Labradors, and if you wish to train your Labrador as a working gundog, again, a working-strain dog is probably a better choice. If you have no real interest in dog sports and like a more heavily built Labrador with a classic Labrador look, then a dog from show lines might suit you better.

If colour is important, you may have less choice. In the UK, for example, there are far fewer chocolate Labradors available from working lines – most are show or pet bred – and the majority of dark yellow (fox-red) Labradors are field bred. So if you want a particular type of dog, you may have to compromise on colour.

Of course, the vast majority of Labradors are first and foremost companions. Show or field, old or young, working gundog or pet, Labradors are loved and treasured in homes up and down the land. The health and welfare benefits to human beings of canine companionship are well documented, but with Labradors those benefits go much further. Living in our midst are thousands of Labradors who, on a daily basis, provide a service so special and so important, it is impossible to put a price on it, or to imagine what life would be like without them.

Fox red Labradors are often from field-bred lines.

Labradors in service

The service we perhaps associate most closely with the Labrador is that provided by guide dogs. The Guide Dogs for the Blind Association was founded in 1931 and we are all familiar with the loyal dogs we see out and about on our streets, leading their owners safely as they go about their daily lives. In fact, guide dogs these days are often Labrador cross-breeds, and there is an enormous diver-sity of *other* service roles in which Labradors abound. Nowhere are the unique talents of these dogs more valuable than in saving and supporting those whose health and happiness depend upon them.

Many Labradors are respected members of our armed services, involved in detecting explosives, but they also play a role in supporting traumatised soldiers and helping to restore them to health. Most of us know that Labradors and other gundogs work with customs officers, helping to reduce the amount of drugs imported illegally into this country. Labradors are also trained to sniff out all kinds of other important substances that may be subject to theft or illegal impor-tation, from metal to money, and are even used by pest-control companies to sniff out bed bugs, a growing problem in many big cities.

Labradors are being trained as lifelong companions for vulnerable young people, including autistic children, and as partners in schools and libraries to help children with reading difficulties. Reading to a calm and friendly dog helps to encourage young children and builds their confidence. Pets as Therapy dogs, many of them Labradors, are taken into nursing homes and hospitals to befriend and support lonely and vulnerable people. Yet other Labradors go to work as search-and-rescue dogs, accompanying their owners at a moment's notice, possi-bly hopping on a plane to travel to earthquake zones or to go to look for missing people on moors and mountains.

In the last few years, we have made extraordinary progress with using dogs in the field of medicine. Labradors have been trained to detect critical changes in blood sugar, and so can become vital partners for people with diabetes. We even have Labradors that can detect tumours in people with cancer. While other breeds of dog are involved in some of these roles, Labradors dominate the list, which really does beg the question – why is the Labrador such an outstandingly successful and useful dog? It isn't just his basic gundog heritage, although clearly that plays a part. There is more to it than that.

Why is the Labrador so successful?

Why is this ten-a-penny, one-on-every-street-corner dog muscling in on just about every field of canine endeavour and taking it by storm? How come the Labrador steals the show every time? Is it just an accident, or a coincidence? Is it the Labrador's happy-go-lucky temperament, his debonair good looks, or the fact that he can charm the dinner off the table?

He's not without faults, after all. He is big, greedy, smelly, clumsy, boisterous, careless and messy; and when young, he can be very destructive. He rips up the designer beds you buy for him, breaks all his toys, digs up the garden and steals from the bin. So why is it we cannot get enough of him?

The answer lies in the Labrador's specific role as a retriever. All gundog work requires a degree of co-operation between the dog and his human partner. Natural instincts to hunt and chase are essential, but so is control. Spaniels that hunt and flush game out of range of the gun, for example, are no use to the hunter. But retrieving requires an even greater depth of partnership. The retriever that carries a bird gently but won't give it back, or one that will not follow directions at a distance, is not going to be a very useful dog. So not only do we need the natural instincts and urges that we breed into our gundogs, we also need them to have a strong desire to communicate with, and be with, a human partner.

The ultimate in teamwork

Many people imagine a working retriever's job as being fairly straightforward. He sees a bird shot, runs over to the area where he saw it fall, picks it up and runs back with it – very nice, but not particularly impressive. Retrievers have a natural ability to mark the point of fall when they see an animal shot, which is honed and refined with training. However, a substantial part of a retriever's job is to fetch game that he didn't see shot. It may be a bird his handler shot while he was retrieving another bird, out of sight; or it may be a bird shot by a different person. Either way, one of the most important roles of the retriever is to fetch a retrieve the approximate location of which is known only by a human being. These are called blind retrieves.

Getting a dog to run blind retrieves reliably and over long distances involves an outstanding piece of teamwork. The job of the handler is to get the dog close enough to the retrieve so that he can find it with his nose. This requires a lot of complex training because the dog has to be directed to the right area, which might be across a river, or through a hedge and across a field, or on the other side of a wood, and this direction is given to the dog by a series of whistles and hand signals, sometimes over distances of hundreds of metres.

A unique blend

What we have done with our Labrador Retrievers, over generations of selective breeding, is create a dog that has an astonishing ability to learn this complex skill, a passion for retrieving that takes him through that learning process, and a desire to co-operate with people that enables that process to take place. It is this unique blend of intelligence, passion and willingness to co-operate that lies at the heart of the Labrador's success in so many walks of life.

It is not surprising that so many people want to share their lives with one of these beautiful, intelligent and trusted animals. Able to morph from hunting partner to household pet and back in the space of a single day, this most affable and willing canine partner has truly earned the nation's vote.

If you are about to bring a Labrador into your life, you have a fantastic journey ahead of you. There will be downs as well as ups but, if you are well prepared, they will be mostly ups. If you haven't quite made up your mind whether or not to bring home a Labrador, the next chapter is especially for you. We're going to take a look at what life with a Labrador is really like!

Labradors' intelligence and loyalty give them a very wide appeal.

2

Are you ready for a Labrador?

Raising and training a Labrador puppy is one of life's great joys, but life with a new Labrador isn't always plain sailing. Many times, new Labrador parents just need the right information and a little support in order to weather some of the common difficulties we all experience with puppies and young dogs. But sometimes, people struggle because they are not quite ready for the commitment of dog ownership, and sometimes because a different type of dog might have been better suited to their family.

In this chapter, I'm going to help you make sure that this is the right time to bring a dog into your life, and that the Labrador is the right breed for you.

Getting wet is all part of the fun when you have a Labrador!

Is this the right time?

If you bring a dog into your home, it won't just change your life – it will change the dynamics of your family. Everyone will be affected, even the family cat. If you have three children under five and twins on the way, you probably don't need me to tell you that now is not a good time to get a dog, although it is surprising just how many people do take on a puppy when their kids are tiny and then struggle to cope. Having a puppy is quite an intense experience, and while some dogs and kids do rub along together very nicely, it can be tough in the early years. Puppies play-bite and have poor bladder control. So you may find yourself alternating between mopping up puddles and drying your children's tears. Small puppies are easily injured by children climbing on them and tripping over them. A toddler, expensive veterinary treatment and a puppy with its leg in plaster do not make a great combination.

A puppy and a small baby may seem a better option, timing-wise. Why not get the baby stage out of the way and have them grow up together? But that can be an even bigger challenge. What seemed like a brilliant plan in your friend's kitchen while you admired her basketful of beautiful Labrador babies, may not seem such a good idea at two in the morning when you are stood in the garden waiting for a puppy to wee by torchlight, while your own baby screams his head off upstairs in his cot.

Consider your lifestyle

Most of us have to work these days, often longer hours than we would like, and some of us have time-consuming hobbies or sports, or are supporting children who are similarly engaged. A dog can be a far bigger problem in this respect than some people anticipate.

In many families in the UK, both parents work full-time up to, and after, the births of their children. Many ordinary homes are empty from around eight in the morning until after four in the afternoon when children start trickling home from school. In residential areas, whole streets may be eerily deserted during the working week and yet in many of these streets, behind each front door lies a dog. Some seem uncomplaining; others howl and bark in protest for hours at a time. We discuss this topic from time to time on my Internet forum, and while a significant proportion of people feel it is wrong for those working full-time to keep a dog, there are clearly those who make a success of it.

The secret seems to lie in being willing to pay for a sufficient level of daycare to keep your dog happy, and to a certain extent in the individual temperament of your dog. A dog is rather like a child – if you have one, you either have to look after it or pay someone else to do it for you. How much daycare you will need depends on whether your dog is a puppy or an adult, and daycare doesn't come cheap.

It is true that, unlike your six-year-old child, you can leave an older dog alone for part of each day, but there is no guarantee that he won't howl or chew things up. You can leave puppies alone for shorter periods of time, but not for hours on end. Some people find that the emotional commitment of owning a dog, having to come home at lunch time each day and walk in the dark each winter morning, far more of a drain than they imagined. It's a tie, a commitment and a big emotional responsibility. If you are ready for that, the rewards are great, but if you are not, they may not be sufficient.

If you don't feel quite ready to be tied down, already have a number of time-consuming hobbies, have just planned an adventure holiday to the Himalayas or are drawn to the idea of canoeing up the Amazon, it might be a good idea to postpone dog ownership for a while. If you think you are ready for this but aren't quite sure, one way to test yourself is to look after a friend's dog for a few days and see how it pans out.

Small puppies need a lot of concentrated effort, so while you may be ready for a dog in a general sense, it isn't a good idea to bring a puppy home in the week before Christmas, or just before your daughter's wedding day, as you simply won't be able to give the puppy the attention he needs.

Is a Labrador the right breed for you?

Once you are certain you are ready for a dog, it is important to consider the particular characteristics of the Labrador, both his physical attributes and his temperament, since these will have an impact on your life, your home and your wallet. Bearing in mind the extraordinary success of the breed, it wouldn't be unreasonable to assume that such a dog was simply the ideal pet for the average family. Of course, in real life, there is no *average* family. Everyone's circumstances are unique in some way or another, and some people's lives are not suited to this large, friendly and athletic dog. Perhaps the first thing to consider is the space around you.

It is possible to raise and keep a Labrador in a flat or apartment but I wouldn't recommend it. Adult Labradors need a good deal of space and exercise, and you really need a secure outdoor area where your dog can answer the call of nature and play, and where you can start some basic training. Indoors, if you decide to use a crate, as many people do nowadays, the crate your Labrador will need will be large, unattractive and may dominate your kitchen for the next year or so. You

Even the friendliest dog requires supervision around young children.

must to be comfortable with this.

Labradors have a distinctive smell, which they like to enhance on occasions by rolling in rotting seagulls or fox poo. If you have a Labrador, you'll also need a hosepipe or similar outdoor device for removing unpleasant smears from your grinning dog. Speaking of water, many Labradors love to swim. However, they don't share our preference for chlorine or water quality – the muddier and smellier the pond, the better. A favourite occupation is lying belly down in a mud puddle, followed by a quick roll. Are you okay with this? Some people like the smell of Labrador body odour, some don't. Whether or not you like it, if you live with a Labrador, you will often smell 'doggy' and so will your home. You won't notice it after a while, but your visitors will.

Labradors have a very dense undercoat, which they deposit profusely on your carpets at intervals throughout the year, usually in spring and autumn, and sometimes in-between. You can hasten the shedding process a little through grooming, but it cannot be avoided. Even with frequent vacuuming, you will have hairy carpets and hairy clothes for several weeks. Unless you are happy to colour co-ordinate your clothes with your dog, you will probably rarely look smart from a distance, and never at close quarters.

Hairy carpets, doggy smells and muddy paws are all part of owning a Labrador, and it's a price that many Labrador owners the world over are happy to pay for the privilege of sharing their lives with one of these beautiful creatures. What is important is that you know what you are getting into, so that you can decide whether or not it is a price that you personally are happy to pay. The next thing to consider is the financial cost of your proposed new family member, above and beyond the actual purchase price.

Fun-loving Labradors have bundles of energy.

Cost

Every dog costs money, but there are extra costs involved in keeping a relatively large dog. Food bills are higher for bigger dogs and this can add up considerably over the course of a year. Big crates cost more than little ones. Labradors need larger beds, collars, bowls and so forth, than smaller dogs. Bigger usually means more expensive.

Boarding-kennel fees and veterinary bills are higher for larger dogs than smaller ones, and insuring a Labrador against ill health, which I recommend you do, will also make a significant dent in your wallet. The costs of attending training classes needs to be considered, too.

A major expense for many Labrador owners lies in securing an outdoor area where the dog can relax and answer the call of nature without constant supervision. Some Labradors will not jump a fence over a metre or so high (four or five feet) but two metres (six feet) is safer. Anything lower than a metre (four feet) is a waste of money, as he may simply sail over the top. You also need to ensure that the dog cannot dig under the fence or push through a hedge. Bear in mind that there are very few hedges that will keep a determined Labrador in, so for most of us, a tall, solid fence, including the gate, is the only option.

Exercise and training

You'll obviously be aware that Labradors need regular exercise. That's part of the fun of owning a dog. Your adult dog, once fit, will happily walk or trot along with you for mile after mile, hour after hour. Walking is fun in the summer and when the weather is good, but you'll need to be committed to walking in all weathers, no matter how tired, bored, ill or stressed you may be. This will probably do you good, but it can be hard to appreciate the health benefits on a dark winter's evening after a long day's work and with a fading torch battery. Exercising your dog will take a sizeable chunk of your time. You need to allow at least an hour each morning or evening, and half an hour at least at the other end of the day. For a considerable part of this time, your dog needs to be engaged in aerobic activity. He needs to be able to run and jump, climb and swim, play Frisbee or retrieve balls to stay healthy and happy. If you have a large garden, some of this activity time can take place at home.

You will also need to be committed to regular daily training sessions to make sure that your dog is under your control. If a Chihuahua jumps up at old ladies or pulls on the lead, it's probably no big deal. A Labrador that lunges after other dogs or jumps on passers-by is a hazard to himself and others. For this reason alone, training is not optional for this breed. Labradors are very intelligent and easily bored, and also need the mental stimulation of regular training. Of course, training is repetitive and takes time and patience. Once your dog is fully trained and mature, he will be a safe and valuable companion to all kinds of people, but while he is growing up, and you are learning together, there may be accidents. So you need to consider any vulnerable people who may be in regular contact with him.

Both males and females are fairly boisterous dogs, especially in the first couple of years, and some young dogs are very clumsy. An adult male Labrador may weigh as much as 36 kilograms (80lb). It is important that you consider the potential impact of this clumsiness on any vulnerable or frail members of your family.

Most Labradors become less boisterous as they grow up.

If you have a toddler or elderly parents, a lively young Labrador can be a problem. You may find that no sooner have you dusted your toddler down and set him back on his feet, than he is bowled over again by his bouncy friend. This can wear a bit thin after a while, and with an elderly person in the house, could be quite dangerous. Once your dog is trained, these are no longer problems, but it bears repeating – training takes time.

A friendly, sociable dog

Labradors are very sociable dogs. They need company and can become miserable and even disturbed if left alone for long periods of time. Home-alone Labradors may howl or bark for prolonged periods of time, or attempt to demolish your fixtures and fittings. A crate may help protect your home for short absences, but you cannot reasonably leave a crated dog on his own for more than four hours. If you want a dog that will be happy to spend long hours on his own, a Labrador may not be the best choice of breed for you.

One final but very important consideration is your hopes with regard to a dog providing extra security for your home. Many people write to me to complain that their dog is not guarding their home. If you want a guard dog, a Labrador is not a great choice. Most will happily offer any burglar a cuddly toy and show him where the TV is. Many Labradors bark rarely, if at all. Mine almost never do.

Decision made

It's a lot to think about, isn't it? Can you cope with the mess? Are you up for training and walking in all weathers? Do you have a garden and can you afford to fence it securely? Can you afford veterinary insurance, vaccinations, training classes and food? Were you hoping for a guard dog? Will you be upset if your dog digs up your flowerbeds? Do you mind a huge crate in your kitchen? These are all questions you need to ask yourself and to answer with honesty. The rewards of life with a Labrador are great, but there is a cost, and if you are well prepared in advance, you will be in a better position to meet it.

The moment you make that decision is an exciting one. 'That's it! We're going to get a Labrador.' But hold on one second. Before you rush to visit your neighbour's new puppies, scour the small ads in the local paper or start browsing the Internet, there is something you need to know. The next decision you make, where you purchase your Labrador and from whom, can have a huge impact on your future. That's why I have devoted the next two chapters to finding and choosing your new best friend.

Finding a new Labrador is one of life's greatest adventures.

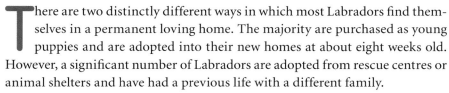

3
Finding your new best friend

There are two distinctly different ways in which most Labradors find themselves in a permanent loving home. The majority are purchased as young puppies and are adopted into their new homes at about eight weeks old. However, a significant number of Labradors are adopted from rescue centres or animal shelters and have had a previous life with a different family.

Depending on the reasons that these rescued dogs were abandoned in the first place, they can be anything from three-month-old pups to elderly dogs of ten years or more. In this chapter, we are going to look at the pros and cons of adopting a rescued Labrador compared with the pros and cons of purchasing an eight-week-old puppy.

Rewards of adopting

When a rescue goes well, there is nothing quite like it. To see an older dog saved from the brink of death and given a new lease of life in a loving family, and to know that you made that happen, is about as good as it gets. It is important to find a good fit between a rescue dog and his future companions. The best rescue centres are experienced at getting this right. They also provide a support system for rescuers and their families once the adoption has taken place, and will take the dog back if the adoption goes wrong.

Many people who adopt an abandoned dog have moral and ethical reasons for doing so. They feel that it is wrong to bring more puppies into the world while dogs are living in shelters. If you feel this way, you will probably be more comfortable adopting a rescue dog than purchasing a puppy. There are practical benefits to adoption, too.

With an older dog, what you see is what you get. If one ear is higher than the other and his tail is on the skinny side, you'll know it. If he has a sweet little habit of lifting one paw when you offer him a treat, you'll know that, too. You might not discover every aspect of his temperament on a first visit, but a good rescue centre will fill you in on the rest. You'll know if he is scared of men, likes to chase cats or dig in the garden. You'll know if he prefers to sleep at the bottom of the stairs, adores other dogs and is picky about his food. A rescue dog usually takes a little while to settle in, and during this time, you'll discover if he likes to 'sing' when you play the piano, shares your dislike of hugging your mother-in-law and enjoys raiding the kitchen bin while you pop out to the shops. Unless your mother-in-law lives with you, these are probably trivial matters that can be managed.

Adopting a dog isn't free. The rescue society will ask for a donation to cover the costs of the adoption process. This will be less than the purchase price of a puppy but, of course, either of these is only a small part of the overall cost of bringing a dog into your life.

Puppies are hard work and need a great deal of attention and supervision, especially in the first few weeks. An older, rescue dog, on the other hand, may well be house trained, probably won't need you to get up in the night, and is unlikely to wet himself if you go out for three or four hours each day.

Children must be taught to treat their dog kindly.

Small children and puppies are not always a good mix. Small puppies play-bite and can be very rough, older puppies are boisterous and clumsy and it is very hard to train a lively young dog with a toddler in tow. Not all dogs that end up in rescue are problem dogs. People die, and get divorced. Perfectly nice dogs can find themselves homeless for absolutely no reason other than plain bad luck. I have known some wonderful, well-behaved rescue dogs that have given their new families nothing but joy. An older rescue dog that has been raised with children and whose temperament is relatively calm and gentle might be the perfect fit for your young family.

Requirements for adoption

Adopting a dog is not just a case of turning up at a kennels and browsing along rows of dogs until you find one you like. To be considered as adoptive parents, you need to demonstrate to the rescue centre that you are suitable carers for one of their dogs. What they want to avoid at all costs is the poor dog being passed from pillar to post and being returned from home after home. For this reason, the rescue organisation will go to some lengths to ensure that you have the right facilities, lifestyle and commitment to take on a dog. This process can seem intrusive at times.

Checking each other
The checking procedures work both ways, and it is crucial that both parties – you and the rescue centre – are totally honest. The society must be honest about the support and help that they offer and about any challenges you will face with the dog they are trying to match to your family. You need to be honest about every aspect of your home situation, and you will need to allow a home visit and interview. Expect to be grilled. A good society will do their level best to ensure that their dogs are not placed in families who cannot cope or are not ready to take on a dog at this point in their lives.

Many rescues will insist on an interview and home check long before you get to meet any of their dogs. Home checkers are often volunteers rather than rescue staff or administrators, but they will have a checklist of questions to ask you. Before you contact your local rescue, make sure you fulfil the basic requirements that the organisation has in place.

A secure garden
Most will expect you to have a secure perimeter around your garden. So you'll need to check that your fence and any gates are dog proof, and that the dog cannot dig under them, or jump over them.

Your other dogs
Many societies won't rehome a dog of any sex to a family with an existing dog that is not neutered. This is often as a result of policies formed before recent research on the effects of neutering (see Chapter 12, Sexual maturity) became available. It may mean that if you don't want to neuter your current dog, you might not be able to adopt from your local rescue. It's probably worth clarifying this point in advance of your home visit.

Someone at home

Another common sticking point for rescue organisations is full-time work, and sometimes part-time work, too. Even if you are prepared to put good daycare arrangements in place, rescue centres are usually reluctant to place dogs in homes where all the family are out at work for part of the day. This is gradually changing and some rescues will look at each case on an individual basis, but, rightly or wrongly, others simply have a blanket ban on owners who work away from home.

Making a match

If all goes well and you are approved by your local rescue, arrangements will be made for you to meet your dog. Some rescues do have dogs that you can visit in kennels, but many home most or all of their dogs with foster carers. Some rescues will offer no choice at all, but simply match you to the dog they think best suits your family. If you are able to visit your new dog with his foster carers, this can be helpful because it means you will be visiting the dog in a home setting. Nowadays, many rescues have Facebook pages and this can be a way of viewing pictures of dogs waiting for homes, and finding out a bit more about them. Bringing a rescue dog home is not quite like bringing a puppy home. In some ways, he will be easier, and in other ways, more challenging.

What to expect from a rescue dog

A strange, adult dog living in your home can seem very odd at first. The responsibility may weigh heavily on you for a while, especially if the dog has some behavioural problems, even if you are well prepared for them. These feelings will pass as the dog settles in and becomes one of the family, and this process can be hastened by hand feeding.

Most of us think of dog food as something that gets poured into a bowl and placed on the floor in front of the dog. He then spends less than five minutes eating it. This is a huge wasted opportunity. Each time a dog is presented with something to eat, it helps to deepen the bond between him and the person feeding him. If he is fed once or twice a day, that is just one or two bonding opportunities. If his entire daily food allowance is divided up and fed at intervals, there could be dozens, even hundreds, of bonding moments each and every day. If you are considering rescue, hand feeding is well worth factoring in to your plans.

Toilet training

Some rescue dogs have spent much of their lives without proper care. They may have been left shut in with their own mess, and may even have lost some of their natural desire to be clean. It is entirely possible to house train an older dog, but it may take some time and patience. It is worth treating any new rescue dog as you would a puppy in this respect, even one that has been toilet trained. So someone will need to be around much of the time to ensure he gets to his designated toilet area at regular intervals, and to reward him profusely for eliminating there. In one way, this is easier than with a puppy, because an older dog has a much greater bladder capacity. In another way, it is harder, because he may have got into bad habits. In time, and with patience, most dogs will come to enjoy being clean and to take responsibility for holding on until they reach the appropriate toilet area.

Recall issues

Recall is often shaky in a rescue dog, and recall is such an important command that it is best to assume a rescue dog will need some retraining. This means factoring in the time to teach a new dog reliably to come to a whistle or call, and making plans for ensuring his safety in the meantime (see Chapter 10, Practical training: the basics). If the rescued dog was trained before, he'll make rapid progress, and if he wasn't, some heart-stopping moments and a good deal of worry will be avoided.

I think that there is probably a time in most dog owners' lives when they are in the right place to take on a rescue dog, and times when they are not. Whether this is the right time for you, is something only you can decide. If you choose to buy a puppy this time around, that does not make you a bad person. There may be a point later on in your life when the time is right for you to give another chance to an abandoned dog.

The benefits of purchasing a puppy

To a certain extent, a puppy is an unknown quantity. You won't know whether or not he'll have his father's rugged good looks or his mother's steady good nature. Although all Labradors share certain characteristics, great variations exist between individuals, even from the same litter. This has to be balanced against the fact that you have tremendous influence over a puppy. You can make sure that he never learns to snatch or to whine for attention. You can be confident that he will never be ill treated or have his willingness to learn or co-operate crushed by poor handling. You can socialise him to perfection so that he never has any reason to fear children, or buses, or men in funny hats. You can start training at an early age and maximise his potential, which is especially important if you want to compete with your dog or to work him on a shoot. You can sometimes do these things with a rescue dog, but in many cases,

You have tremendous influence over your new puppy.

it will take time and patience to eradicate bad habits first.

I am a huge supporter of rescue, but it is important to recognise that rescue is not right for every family, and not every rescue dog is an easy dog. It is not unusual for me to hear from people who have taken on rescue dogs and are now in despair. Some rescue dogs come with deep-seated problems, causing immense heartbreak to the families who take them in and find themselves totally out of their depth. Some dogs from rescue centres may have uncertain temperaments, soil repeatedly in the house, run away when let off the lead, or obsessively chase rabbits, deer, cyclists or cars. Some may be destructive in the house, destroying fixtures and fittings. Some are terrified of men, or of other dogs, or children. Some will be prone to loud or constant barking. These are difficult problems for even experts to solve, and dogs that have them may be best suited to those with both experience in dealing with challenging dogs and a significant amount of free time to devote to rehabilitating their older Labrador.

Many rescue dogs have only minor problems (if they have problems at all), but from the potential owner's point of view, they are avoidable by the simple expedient of purchasing and carefully raising and training a puppy from scratch. For some families, especially those with no experience of dog ownership, or who don't quite meet the criteria for adoption from their local shelter, a puppy may be a better bet.

Aside from practical advantages, great pleasure is to be had in nurturing and raising your own dog from puppyhood, in helping to shape his character and in watching him grow and mature into an adult. So while it can be very reward-ing and often surprisingly easy to raise and care for a rescued dog, there is no shame in wanting to raise a puppy, at least once in your lifetime.

If you decide that now is the right time for you to rescue an abandoned dog, you can find a list of Labrador Rescue Societies at the back of this book. If you decide that now is the right time for a puppy, the information in the next chapter is for you. One of the disadvantages of buying a puppy is that you have no way of knowing *for certain* how it will turn out in terms of health and temperament. However, you have far more influence over these two important factors than you might think. Let's find out how you can give your new friend the best chance of growing into a happy and healthy adult, by making some wise choices before you buy your puppy.

Let your pup visit lots of different locations when she is young.

4

How to buy a healthy puppy

Wellness is so precious and so inextricably entwined with happiness that we all wish to protect our puppies' health. We will be looking at how you can keep your Labrador fit and well in Chapter 7, Your Labrador's health, but the foundations of good health are laid long before you bring your puppy home.

Each year, far too many new Labrador-puppy owners go through the devastating process of learning that their young dog or puppy has an unpleasant disease

Healthy puppies have the best chance of growing up to be happy dogs.

or disorder, often one that will permanently affect the quality of his life and make huge holes in the family finances. Yet, in many cases, this disaster could have been avoided with the right information and preparation. The purpose of this chapter is to make sure that your family brings home a puppy with a bright and healthy future, by choosing his parents wisely. For more information on genetic diseases, see Chapter 14, Breeding from your Labrador.

Your puppy's genetic heritage

Genes contain the code or instructions that tell your Labrador's body how to develop. There are genes that make your Labrador black or brown, genes that determine the power of his urge to retrieve, genes that make sure his heart works properly, and so on. When the code inside a gene becomes damaged or faulty in some way, it sends out the wrong information and causes disorders that can then be passed down from one generation to the next. This isn't just a Labrador problem. Within *every* gene pool lurk some unpleasant faulty genes, which may remain hidden and harmless for generations. This cloaking effect happens because genes come in pairs and, in many cases, a healthy gene, when paired with a faulty one, will override it. Let's see how that works.

Your puppy's eyesight

We have a bad gene in our Labrador population that causes premature blindness – a disease called progressive retinal atrophy (PRA). Let's say your puppy inherits a faulty, PRA-causing gene from his dad. Provided he also gets a healthy gene from his mum, the faulty gene will remain switched off and silent, and your puppy won't go blind at a young age. With simple recessive diseases, *two matching faulty genes* are required in order for the disease to develop, and that can happen only when two dogs carrying the fault are mated together.

Happily, genetic tests have been developed for several diseases, including PRA, that exist in our Labrador gene pool. Some other diseases are more complex.

Your puppy's joints

Other health problems that can affect Labradors are not caused by a single gene, but by a group of genes, or by a group of genes acting together with some environmental influences. One of the most common health problems to affect Labradors in this way is hip dysplasia, a potentially crippling malformation of the hip joint that can lead to severe pain, lameness and arthritis at a young age.

Hip dysplasia is a painful condition that causes lifelong problems for the dog and often requires expensive surgical treatment in order to maintain a reasonable quality of life for the sufferer. The potential for the disease can be detected on X-rays, and all good Labrador breeders will have the parents of any puppies they produce tested. X-rays of the dogs' hips are sent off to be assessed by the British Veterinary Association (BVA) and the dogs are allocated a score.

An evaluation of hip scores in 2010 showed that Labrador hips are slowly improving as a result of these tests. If *more* people would score their dogs before breeding, and select only the dogs with the best hips, improvement would be swifter. If more puppy buyers would ask to see certificates, more breeders would test. A similar scheme is in operation for elbow dysplasia, and all you need to do in order to help ensure the health of your puppy is to ask to see the certificates before you buy.

Other inherited conditions

Some rather less common diseases have been identified in our Labrador gene pool, and tests are available to detect these, too. Two that you might want to consider asking for are tests for centronuclear myopathy (CNM), and exercise-induced collapse (EIC). They work like the PRA tests in that if one parent is tested clear, your puppy will be protected.

How does this affect you?

The reason I am giving you this information is because if your puppy is still an idea in your mind, or a plan not yet come to fruition, if he is not yet sitting in your lap, and hasn't yet wriggled his way into your heart, you can choose to limit his chances of ever getting hip dysplasia, or elbow dysplasia, and you can make it impossible for him to get PRA blindness. These are not rare conditions. Many Labradors suffer from them every year. You can and should help to make your puppy safer by selecting his parents carefully.

Thousands of Labrador puppies are born in the UK and the USA each year. It is estimated that 50 to 60 per cent of these puppies are born to hip-scored parents, which means that nearly half of puppies are born to parents that are *not tested at all*. In the UK, all these puppies can *still be registered* with the Kennel Club. You could buy such a puppy with an excellent pedigree tomorrow. The fact that your puppy has a pedigree is no protection. Choosing your puppy from tested parents with good scores will help to reduce the risk that he will suffer from this disease. Failing to do so could cast a shadow over the next ten years of your life. I cannot over-emphasise the importance of this simple precaution. You can find out more about these schemes and the scores you should be looking for in Chapter 14, Breeding from your Labrador.

Where should your puppy come from?

The person who breeds the litter your puppy comes from has a lot of control over your puppy's future well-being – not just physically, but mentally, too. The breeder is responsible for ensuring that the puppies get off to a great start

Your puppy's breeder can influence his future, for better or worse.

with socialisation, the process that ensures your puppy will not grow up fearful of normal everyday objects and experiences. This cannot happen if your puppy and his siblings are shut away in an outdoor kennel around the clock.

Breeding healthy, happy puppies requires some knowledge, effort, funding and commitment. Don't be tempted to purchase a puppy from someone who lacks the resources to do the job properly. Choose wisely.

Finding a responsible breeder

It is tempting to leap to the free ads on Google to begin your puppy search, but this is a bad idea. Most responsible Labrador breeders would never advertise on general-purpose Internet puppy-sales sites. Many don't advertise at all because they have a constant waiting list for their puppies. So how can you go about finding one?

The Kennel Club has a list of Labrador breed clubs in the UK. This is your starting point for building a list of contacts. Visit each club's website and look at the committee members. Many of these people are themselves breeders. If they no longer breed, they will be able to put you in touch with someone who does.

If you have a specific role in mind for your Labrador, as a working gundog, for example, or show dog, or you want him to compete in agility, you'll need to find a breeder of the right strain or type of Labrador for that purpose. Each person you contact will be happy to explain which type of Labrador they specialise in and to recommend an alternative breeder if their dogs are not suited to your purpose. There may be some give-away letters next to their name: FT, for example, stands for field trial; and WT for working test. Make a list of contacts to approach from each club, and then phone or email them.

Following the stud-dog trail

If the breeder you contact has no puppies available and none on the way, ask about stud dogs. Many breeders will have one or more male dogs available at stud and a list of all the bitches their dog has been mated to. Enquire about recent matings and get contact details for the bitches' owners. Bear in mind that membership of a breed club is not a guarantee of integrity. You will still need to be diligent with your checks, because, sadly, some breeders will allow their champion dogs to mate with bitches that have *no* health clearances.

What to ask the breeder

Once you have made contact with a breeder who has a litter of puppies, don't book a visit until you have got the correct answers to some important questions. Have a notepaper and pen ready. Ask the breeder:

- **What are the father's hip and elbow scores?**
- **What are the mother's hip and elbow scores?**

In the UK at the time of writing, the total hip score for each of your puppy's parents should be less than twelve and the two hips should be balanced (ideally no more than two or three points difference between them). Elbows should be 0/0. For up-to-date regional information, contact your country's Kennel Club.

- **What is the date of the father's most recent eye examination?**
- **What is the date of the mother's most recent eye examination?**

Both parents should have had an eye examination in the last twelve months. They may be DNA Optigen tested, which is great, and, if so, one parent should be clear and neither parent should be *affected*.

- **When were the puppies born?**
- **When will the puppies be ready to go to their new homes?**

There should be eight weeks between these two dates. A responsible breeder will not try to sell puppies at six weeks old. Early separation is bad for the puppies – they need to remain with their mother and siblings in order to develop properly. Puppies separated too young are likely to bite more, and may be touch sensitive. A common excuse for selling puppies prematurely is that the mother's milk has dried up, or even 'the bitch has died'. This is probably untrue and is irrelevant as puppies are weaned at six weeks – they need the proximity of their siblings and mother, not her milk.

- **Will the puppies be registered on the Kennel Club breed register?**

If your puppies are advertised as pedigree Labradors, they should be registered with the Kennel Club. Failure to register a pedigree dog can be an indication that the breeder has broken one of the conditions of registration. For example, the breeder might have bred the bitch to a close relative; the bitch might be too young or too old, or have had too many litters, or be unregistered for any of these reasons. At worst, the bitch might have been stolen.

If you are already aware that the puppy you are buying is not purebred and are happy with that, you need to be aware that this will exclude you from participating in a range of Kennel Club activities, including all working-gundog competitions and the show ring. If your puppy is a first cross with another pedigree breed – Poodle, for example – you still need to make sure that both parents have all the correct health clearances for their breed.

- **Are the puppies kennelled or do they live indoors?**

There is nothing wrong with a litter of puppies being born in a properly equipped and maintained kennel. But, if your puppy has been born in a kennel, you need to ask the breeder how much time the puppies spend indoors with the family. This is important. All puppies need to be exposed to normal family life, and that means regular daily contact with human beings and the home environment.

- **How many dogs do you have?**

This is another important question and the answer should generate more questions from you. If the breeder has one bitch, she is probably a family pet; several bitches may indicate a serious hobby breeder, which can be a good thing as such breeders are usually very experienced and often provide lifetime support

Spotting a bad breeder is not always easy.

for their puppy buyers. However, there is also a risk that you have come across a puppy farmer. We'll look at puppy farming in a bit more detail in a moment. The next thing you need to confirm with *this* breeder is whether he/she shows his/her dogs, or works them in the shooting field. Either of these interests will suggest that this is not a puppy farmer, but someone who genuinely loves, and interacts with, their dogs.

The question-and-answer session goes both ways, of course, and long before you get to this point, a good breeder will have some searching questions for you.

What the breeder should ask you

Most breeders will want to know what you want the puppy for. If it is a pet you want, that is okay, although some working-line breeders will try to find working homes for *all* their puppies and, in any case, should point out that you will need to keep your working-bred dog well occupied, both physically and mentally.

Your breeder will want to know if you have ever owned a dog before, and, if not, they will question you about your expectations of the breed and its requirements. They will want to know if you have any children, and you may find that some breeders are not prepared to sell a puppy to homes where there are children under five years old. This is simply because families with very small children are more likely to struggle with a Labrador puppy and even to return it, or pass it on to someone else.

You will also be asked about your home and garden. Most Labrador breeders won't sell to buyers who don't have a securely fenced and reasonably sized garden. There will be lots of other questions as your breeder tries to get a feel for the kind of person you are. Don't be offended; this is all a very good sign that your breeder is caring and responsible.

Sometimes, despite a great deal of care on the part of puppy buyers, it is possible to get to this point and for puppy buyers to be completely unaware that they are, in fact, dealing with a puppy farm.

Recognising a puppy farm

You may have heard that puppy farms are squalid places where dogs are kept in terrible conditions, but this is not always the case. Many puppy farms are well organised and clean. They may be licensed by the local authority, their pedigree puppies will probably be registered with the Kennel Club and the dogs in them will appear to be healthy and well kept. Just because the premises you visit are clean, tidy and licensed does not mean it isn't a puppy farm.

What defines a puppy farm is that the *primary purpose* of the bitches who live there is the production of puppies, and that those bitches lack any meaningful relationship or bond with a human being. This situation is not always an easy one for an inexperienced puppy buyer to recognise.

Many puppy farmers will bring a bitch and her puppies into their kitchen for viewing purposes, so that it *seems* like a family environment. And, of course, some reputable breeders kennel their dogs, so you can't rely on the absence or presence of kennelling as your guide. One give-away is that the puppy farmer almost always deals in more than one breed of dog, and sometimes five or six. If you seem unsure about a puppy, you may be offered a different breed. A puppy farmer may well be advertising more than one litter at a time, and probably (but not always) won't have any health certificates for any of them.

Why you should not buy from a puppy farm·

A puppy-farm bitch is kept solely for breeding, and will be discarded (rehomed or destroyed) when her breeding career is over. The puppies themselves are likely to be less well handled and socialised than they should be, and necessary health tests are unlikely to have been carried out on their parents, as they undermine profits.

Puppies need to have been exposed to regular handling and a family environment. This is crucial for their mental development and to ensure that they grow up confident and free from aggression or phobias. Your puppy-farm puppy can end up costing you a whole lot more in behavioural consultations than the money you pay to bring him home. Veterinary attention on a puppy farm may have been minimal, and defects in individual puppies are unlikely to be pointed out to you. Aftercare on puppy farms does not exist. If you return the puppy because he is sick, he will probably be put to sleep. Everything is about profit.

Other dubious sources of puppies

A pet shop or market is one of the worst places to purchase your new companion. There is usually no provenance with a pet-shop puppy, and the chances are he is surplus stock from a puppy farm, stolen or brought in from abroad. You won't know where he came from, his parents won't have been health tested and he could have all kinds of emotional and physical problems. In time, these will become your problems.

You won't get your money back if your puppy dies, or any kind of support if he gets sick. Buying puppies from market stalls is not a question of rescuing them from an awful life. On the contrary, another puppy will replace yours tomorrow, so you are effectively perpetuating a horrible trade in puppies that causes suffering to both the pups and their parents.

If you have a friend or neighbour who has a litter of puppies, and you know the bitch well, it may be very tempting to buy a pup. Do be sure to apply the same criteria as you would to any other breeder. Apart from the heartbreak of a sick puppy, it can cause a terrible rift between friends if something that the breeder could and should have avoided goes wrong down the line.

Choosing your puppy

Once you have located a litter and chatted to the breeder, visiting is the next step in the process, and it's a very exciting one. Most breeders will allow visitors when the pups are around four or five weeks old. By this time, they are up on their legs, getting out and about, and their little personalities are starting to appear.

The first thing to mention is that you may not have a choice. That would be because either there is only one puppy left, or the breeder prefers to allocate the puppies to the families he/she thinks will be best suited to them. Very often, all the puppies in a well-bred litter will be spoken for quite early on, sometimes before they are even born, although one puppy may come back on the market a little later if a family drop out. So it is not something to worry about if only one or two puppies are left to choose from in a litter of eight or nine pups; and there is no reason to suppose that the remaining puppy is any worse than the others in any respect. The fact is that, in terms of temperament, it is almost impossible to pick the 'best' puppy in a litter. They will all change immeasurably over the coming weeks and months, and the quietest may turn out to be the most outgoing. I have known seriously successful Field Trial breeders freely admit that they never pick their own puppy from a litter. They just let their puppy buyers choose, keep the last one for themselves and proceed to turn him into a champion.

The key point to remember is that if you have done your homework to this point, if you have picked a good breeder who has bred for the right reasons and with the right health checks, all the puppies in the litter will probably be equally great companion dogs. Try not to worry if your breeder wants to allocate puppies to families. The breeder does, after all, know the puppies better than anyone at this point; so if anyone can make the right choice, it is probably the breeder. If you do have a choice, you may need to decide between a dog and a bitch.

Dog or bitch?

You will read all kinds of claims for personality differences between dogs and bitches but, by and large, they are not relevant. Most Labradors, male or female, are friendly, confident, outgoing dogs, not prone to fighting or aggression.

It goes without saying that female dogs can get pregnant unless spayed, which is an expensive operation and not without side effects. They come into season at around six-monthly intervals, at which time they have a bloody vaginal discharge, which lasts for around three weeks. During this time, your bitch is very attractive to male dogs.

Male dogs are not without their own issues, which include taking a keen interest in any unspayed bitches in your neighbourhood during their fertile period. You can find out more about the pros and cons of owning a dog of either gender in Chapter 12, Sexual maturity. But, in all honesty, there is little to choose between the sexes and I find both genders equally pleasant company.

If this will be your second dog and your first is not neutered, you will probably want a puppy of the same sex – separating an on-heat bitch and an entire male is a challenging and difficult task, which both dogs will conspire to disrupt. And if you think early neutering will get around the problem, you might change your mind after reading the latest evidence (again, see Chapter 12, Sexual maturity).

One dog or two?

Occasionally, an inexperienced or irresponsible breeder will encourage or even suggest that you take two puppies rather than one, ostensibly so that they will keep each other company. There are several problems with adopting litter-mates together, the first of which is that they may bond with one another to the detriment of the bond with the owner, and there is a tendency for one littermate to bully the other. This is so common that there is a name for it – littermate syndrome. Two puppies have to be trained separately, which is very time consuming. While they might get you through the first couple of nights more peacefully, you could be stacking up trouble for yourself in the weeks and months to come.

Which puppy is best?

The important point here is that if you have done your homework up to this point, and chosen a responsible breeder, it really isn't necessary to worry about which is the best puppy. If this is a good litter, all the puppies will be confident, friendly and healthy. A good breeder will point out any defects that might affect the puppy's potential in the show ring or in the field – a large white patch on the chest, for example, won't affect your dog as a gundog, but will eliminate him from the show ring, and misaligned teeth will be a problem in either case. If you lift up your puppy's lips gently, you can make sure that the bottom teeth fit snugly just behind the top ones. Stroke your fingers gently around his tummy to check for lumps – some puppies have an umbilical hernia, which in mild cases will resolve itself, but is probably best avoided. Apart from this, there is little you can do at this point to distinguish future champions from future problem dogs. If you can, take an experienced person with you to advise. Otherwise, it is largely a case of accepting that you are not an expert, trusting in your choice of breeder and picking the pup that appeals to you most.

What if you are not happy?

It is very important to trust yourself if you are not happy with what you see when you arrive at the breeder's home. Even if he/she sounded wonderful on the phone, and answered all your questions correctly, you still need to make a judgement based on what you see. If the puppies seem thin, nervous, pot-bellied, listless or dirty, or if the kennels are uncared for, make an excuse and leave. If the bitch is not delighted to see you, giving you a tail-wagging welcome, walk away. The temperament of your puppy will be a combination of the effort you put in to socialisation and the temperament of his parents. For him to have the best chance of being happy and confident, he should have a great set of genes. Remember, there is always another litter, and you should never buy a puppy because you feel sorry for it.

If all goes well, as it should, and your breeder and the puppies are everything you had hoped for, then it's time to put down a deposit and arrange to come back to collect the pup when he is eight weeks old. Don't forget to view the puppy's health clearances and KC registration documents if you have not already done so.

Your new puppy

It should be said that choosing a puppy wisely is not a guarantee of a perfect outcome. Plenty of people mess up nice, well-bred puppies, which is partly why so many dogs end up in rescue. One of the objectives of this book is to help make sure you don't mess up *your* dog.

With that in mind, the next two chapters concentrate on puppy rearing. We'll be helping you survive the first few weeks with a new Labrador puppy, and showing you how to cope with some common puppy problems.

5

Surviving the first few weeks

There is frequently a mismatch between what people expect life to be like with a new puppy in the house, and the reality of living with an eight-week-old Labrador. For the most part, we cope better with life's challenges if we are prepared for them, so, in this chapter, I want to give you some idea of what to expect from a new puppy. We will also talk about basic puppy care and your two main challenges for the next few weeks – getting started with house-training and socialisation.

As many families today have to juggle dog and child care with their careers, we'll also be looking at how to combine your *puppy's* needs with *your* obligation to earn a living, and how to cope when life with a puppy gets a bit too much.

What to expect from your new puppy

We all know that Labradors are friendly, clever dogs, and we often expect that Labrador puppies will be easy to train. We assume that our puppy will listen to what we say, come when we call him and want to please us. These things come with time. In the meantime, some aspects of your new puppy's behaviour may be a bit of a shock.

Crying
Most new puppies have never slept alone. If asked to sleep alone on the first night in their new home, they usually cry. A small puppy can make a surprisingly loud noise, so, unless you live in a mansion, you will be able to hear him. Your neighbours may well be able to hear him, too. One way around this is to have the puppy sleep next to your bed for the first few nights, in a deep-sided box or carry crate.

Puppies do need to learn to cope with being alone for short periods of time, but this can wait until he has got over the initial shock of moving home. Young puppies learn to cope best with alone time if it is introduced gradually over the next few days and weeks, and if it never becomes excessive.

Poor bladder control

Eight-week-old puppies have eight-week-old bladders, and only a minimum of control over them. A few new puppies can last six or seven hours at night without a wee, but many cannot do this until they are around ten weeks old. If you crate your puppy at night, expect to get up in the middle of the night to take him outside for a wee, for up to two weeks, sometimes longer, and expect no more lay-ins for a while. During the daytime, small puppies will need frequent trips to their outdoor toilet area. Some will last an hour or so in-between, but many cannot. So, if you are going back to work, or want to leave your puppy for three to four hours before he is five or six months old, you need to arrange for someone else to take care of him during the day. We'll look at house training in more detail in a moment. The point here is to expect very little control from your puppy to begin with and expect to supervise him a great deal.

Biting

Most people know that puppies nip when teething. They are less likely to expect tearful children who can't play with, or even stroke, the puppy because he wriggles and bites so hard. Fierce growling and biting during play is completely normal for small puppies! If your puppy bites hard enough to make your eyes water, and snarls at you or tugs at your clothes, this does not mean he is aggressive or abnormal in some way. There is help in the next chapter if you find that your puppy's biting is getting out of hand, but the key to success is briefly to end all play and interaction with the puppy just as soon as he starts getting rough, and then redirect the biting on to a tug toy.

Chewing

Labradors are often particularly 'mouthy' as puppies, so expect your puppy to destroy anything he can get in his mouth. Expect this to continue well past his first birthday. In fact, many young Labradors become particularly destructive towards the end of the first year, especially when bored. Some even chew the skirting boards, rip plaster from the walls and tear up carpets in their homes. These problems are more likely if the dog is spending far too much time alone. There is no point in getting into a conflict over destructive behaviour. A certain amount is normal, and it will pass in time. When left alone in the house, many young Labradors need to be either crated or penned until well past their first birthday if the house and its contents are to survive intact.

Communication problems

Puppies and people communicate differently. Puppies are quite good at recognising body language, hand signals and posture, for example, but they are poor at interpreting our vocalisations. People often say to me, 'My puppy doesn't listen when I tell him to …' This is normal. Dogs naturally communicate with their bodies, not their voices. This means that you will need to train your puppy

Your new puppy doesn't yet speak your language.

carefully to understand your verbal cues, rather like teaching someone a new language. I'll explain how to do this in the training chapters later on.

People love to show affection through cuddling, and often expect puppies to enjoy being hugged. Cuddling is not a natural behaviour for dogs and many puppies will wriggle wildly at first if held firmly or for long. All dogs need to learn to tolerate being cuddled, so that they can be safe around people, many of whom will presume that dogs enjoy it. This is doubly important with Labradors because everyone assumes they are friendly and huggable. To stop your puppy wriggling when he is picked up, hold him firmly but gently until he is calm, and wait for all wriggling to cease *before* placing him back on the floor.

Supervision and restriction

New puppy owners often give their puppy the freedom to go anywhere he wants to go in their home. However, watching and supervising a puppy is hard work. There is no way you will be able to remain enthusiastic about this for weeks on end if you never get a break. If your puppy has access to your entire home, you will be worn out by the end of the first day. One of the secrets to a relaxing and enjoyable puppyhood, for you and your puppy, is restricted access. This can usually be achieved with the help of one or two baby gates. Restricted access is also important when it comes to getting your puppy clean and dry.

Principles of house-training

Your puppy has a very powerful and useful natural instinct to keep his nest clean. In the wild, this instinct helps to keep the sleeping area, occupied by cubs or pups, free from pathogens and parasites. What this means for you is that your puppy won't empty his bowels or bladder in his nest unless he is physically unable to hold on any longer. So provided you don't leave your puppy in his nest for longer than he can physically cope, if he cannot leave his *nest*, he won't empty himself. One way to ensure the puppy *cannot* leave his nest is to put it inside a small crate.

Accidents are highly likely if the puppy is left with a full bladder for very long. If you leave him in his crate for too long, he will wet his bed. Eating a meal increases the pressure in your puppy's belly, and is likely to increase his need to empty his bladder. In addition, certain activities are likely both to increase this need and to make him forget any toilet training that he may have learned so far.

High-risk points

High-risk activities include any that create arousal, such as fear or excitement. If your puppy is a bit scared, or if he is having a great game, he is likely to need to empty his bladder, and also more likely to miss the signal that his bladder is full, until it becomes so intense that he has to go *right there and then*. Your job is to make sure that the puppy gets to his toilet area before his need to empty his bladder becomes overwhelming, and to help him gradually learn to space out his toilet trips as he gains increasing control over it.

By the time your puppy arrives in your home, he will have a bit more control over his bowels than he does over his bladder, but he still won't be able to hold on for very long. Fortunately, most puppies tend to empty their bowels after eating, so provided you take him to his toilet area after each meal, you shouldn't have too many accidents. Small puppies have short memories. He may have used his toileting area quite regularly for a week or two but that doesn't mean he will remember to use it every time. He is going to need some help and some reminders for a while yet.

Building good habits

Puppies are creatures of habit, and love to go to the toilet in places where they have been to the toilet before. This is both a curse and a blessing – a curse because if your puppy has an accident on your best rug, he'll probably try to empty himself on the rug next time you take your eyes off him; a blessing because once you get him used to using his designated toilet area, he'll be happy to do so over and over again.

Many puppies like to wee on a soft surface, such as a carpet or grass. Obviously, grass is preferable, but you can teach your puppy to wee on any outdoor surface if you wish. The answer to the problem of accidental toileting, and the likelihood of repeated accidents, is to keep puppies off tempting and difficult-to-clean surfaces, such as carpets, at least for the first few weeks, and to clean up any accidents very thoroughly indeed. Remember, dogs can detect minute traces of body fluids with their amazing sense of smell. Cleaning fluids need to be ammonia free because the smell of ammonia, which is present in urine, may tempt the puppy to re-use the scene of the crime.

Baby gates are a great way to keep your puppy in selected parts of the house where floors are washable. I use them until puppies are around six months old. Each time your puppy has emptied himself outdoors, you will have a little window of time in which you won't have to watch him so closely. This little window will get bigger each week. At other times, a small crate (small enough so that the puppy cannot leave his nest) is a good way to supervise a puppy when you cannot watch him closely. He won't wee in the crate unless you leave him for too long. Remember that new puppies may need to wee at half-hourly intervals at certain times of the day, so make crate times short and sweet. If you have to leave a puppy for any significant length of time on a regular basis, you'll need to use the old-fashioned system of newspaper or puppy pads down on the floor.

Before we move on to socialisation, let's sum up key house-training principles.

- **Give your puppy lots of opportunities to toilet in the right place.**
- **Watch out for high-risk times and supervise more closely.**
- **Clean up any accidents thoroughly with ammonia-free detergent.**
- **Keep puppies off carpets for the first few months.**

Socialising your puppy

Socialisation is the other key task for you during the next week or two. This is the process that helps ensure your puppy grows up friendly and fearless. Socialisation is important because it makes dogs safe. Aggression in dogs is nearly always rooted in fear, and socialisation prevents dogs from becoming fearful.

Like most animals, adult dogs are naturally wary of unfamiliar experiences. Sudden noises, shapes and sounds that seem alien to them are treated as potentially dangerous. This is a perfectly healthy defence mechanism. The way we get around this is to expose puppies to all manner of experiences before this beware-of-unfamiliarity response sets in. Unfortunately, that doesn't give us much time, because the period during which puppies are very accepting of new experiences, and very friendly to all and sundry, is coming to an end by around three months of age. After that, socialisation is a slower process.

What you need to do, therefore, is to get your puppy socialised as thoroughly and quickly as possible. This means taking him to lots of new places on a daily basis. It can be quite challenging, especially if you are very busy, but it needs to be done. He should meet different people – men, women and especially children. Take him to busy streets, railway stations, pet shops. Stand outside schools and supermarkets with him at busy times of day. Make sure he meets people wearing hats and people in wheelchairs. Let him meet noisy, clanking vehicles with flashing lights. Stand at the roadside and watch cars go by. Invite lots of people to stroke him and feed him. Whatever you do, don't shut him away at home during these vital few weeks. And, yes, that does mean he needs to go outdoors before his course of vaccinations is complete. So you are going to have to carry him and keep him off the ground until it is safe for him to be down on the floor, and then, once he is fully vaccinated, you need to repeat the whole process with your puppy at ground level – because, let's face it, the world is a very different place down there!

Combining a puppy with work

If you are going to leave a small puppy alone for more than an hour or so during the day, you should not crate him. The risk of him having to soil his bed is too great. Instead, you will need to provide him with a substantial puppy pen. Inside the pen, put his bed, or a small crate with the door open, and away from that he will need a water bowl and some newspaper or puppy pads (you can buy these) for him to wee on.

Labrador puppies need outdoor space and room to play.

It is important to take as much time off work as you can when your puppy arrives, so that you can get to know him, and get house-training off to a good start. If you will eventually be back at work full-time, you need to make some daycare arrangements to prevent your dog becoming lonely and possibly noisy or destructive as a result. Everyone's situation is different, but a friend or dog walker who exercises your dog at midday can work well for an older dog. Young puppies need more attention than that – someone, whether friend, family member or professional, to play with your puppy at home. Another good option is a place (full- or part-time) in a responsible daycare centre, so that your dog has company on a daily basis. Many working-dog parents use a combination of these services.

No one can force you to make these kind of provisions, but I strongly recommend that you do. Aside from the sadness of the dog that is left home alone all week, leaving a Labrador in this way can be a recipe for disturbed behaviour and a whole raft of related problems.

Feeding and growth

Most of our feeding practices are about getting the right nutrients into the puppy while avoiding upset tummies. Information on feeding your Labrador is to be found in Chapter 8, Daily care of your Labrador, but here are a few extra guidelines for puppies:

- Don't change diets suddenly, or when your puppy has been stressed. Feed your new puppy exactly what the breeder was feeding, and make any changes, such as switching brands, gradually over the space of a few days.
- Divide your puppy's daily food allowance into several small portions. Feeding too much at one sitting causes diarrhoea.
- Don't make your puppy fat. Fat puppies may grow too fast and get joint problems as a result. People worry that their puppy is not eating enough or is hungry, but the reality is that Labrador puppies are always hungry. If you feed your puppy to appetite, he will get fat. He should have a waist, and while you don't want to see his ribs, you should be able to feel them if you press your hands along his sides.
- Don't give your puppy milk. Feeding puppies on milk and cereal was common practice many years ago but we now know that cow's milk is not well suited to puppies and may cause diarrhoea. You can buy

replacement bitches' milk, but an eight-week-old puppy is actually weaned and doesn't need milk at all. He needs a raw-meaty diet or a good-quality puppy kibble. We look at these two options in Chapter 8, Daily care of your Labrador.

- Avoid household scraps unless you are very knowledgeable about canine nutrition. A lot of people ask me how to feed dogs on vegetarian diets, and my personal opinion is that you should not attempt this. Puppies need a very well-balanced diet to grow up strong and healthy. Complete puppy kibbles contain all the nutrients your pup needs to develop a healthy body, and are often the best choice for new puppy owners.

Exercise and play

When we bring a Labrador into our lives, we expect our new routine to feature regular daily walks, but before you grab your hat and coat, let's talk about what your puppy needs. The kind of exercise an adult Labrador requires is not appropriate for a puppy and may even be harmful. Three- or four-month-old puppies need no formal exercise at all, just opportunities to romp around in your garden or in safe areas outdoors, and to learn to trot along after you. You may have heard of the five-minute rule. This is a guideline frequently given to new puppy owners to prevent them from over-exercising their pups. It refers to the puppy's age, and states that for every month, the puppy needs just five minutes walking per day. According to this rule, a seven-month-old puppy would need thirty-five minutes of walking per day. It must be emphasised that this is a guideline, and there is no specific evidence to support it. It also refers to formal exercise when the puppy is taken for a walk, and has no option but to keep up, rather than to periods of play at home, when the puppy can stop whenever he is tired. It's common sense, really. The fear is that the puppy's soft bones, especially the development of his joints, might be harmed through excessive exercise, and there is evidence that puppies that are allowed to climb steps and stairs before three months of age may be more likely to develop joint problems later on.

Playing with children or excitable adults is where some families get into trouble with young puppies. Puppy-play rules are very different from human rules and puppies can get very overexcited if allowed to play rough games with people. Try to steer children away from physical rough-and-tumble play with your puppy, and towards training exercises and games that involve the puppy using his brain. Physically separate (using barriers or gates) puppies and children under five unless you are closely supervising.

Coping with the puppy blues

Bringing a new life into your home is a massive change, no matter how prepared you may be. It has a significant effect on every member of the family. Sometimes, after the excitement of the first few days has worn off, and tiredness has set in, we can find ourselves feeling a bit down.

House-training may be more of a struggle than you anticipated, and you may be wondering when the biting and growling is ever going to end. With the build-up to your puppy's arrival, it is inevitable that you are going to come down to earth with a bit of a bump at some point. Lack of sleep can eat away at your patience and sense of humour. Even so, after months of planning and longing for your puppy, you may feel that now your dream has come true, you have no right to complain about how annoying your puppy is becoming.

Friends may have little sympathy. They think you are ungrateful. 'Give him to us,' they demand, half seriously. 'We'd love him.' And you are secretly tempted to do just that. Only your determination not to be a failed puppy owner prevents you.

If you feel like this, you are probably just experiencing a touch of the puppy blues. It is perfectly normal to mourn your previous life, with no ties or responsibilities. You are not the first person secretly to wish you'd never thought of having a puppy.

For most people, these feelings slip away gradually over the next few weeks. So hang on in there for a while, because you probably will adjust, and help is at hand. Right now, your best friends are knowledge and sleep. Arm yourself with information. Accept all offers of help, and in a few weeks, possibly just a few days, all will be well again.

Summary of your puppy's daily needs

Let's have a look now at what is involved in the day-to-day care of a new puppy over the next few weeks.

From 8–10 weeks of age: Your new puppy needs a lot of attention and companionship. For the first few days, your home is a stranger's home, and he may be very upset to be left alone there. You need either to arrange for time off work so that

The first few days at home can be quite a challenge!

you can be with him for *much of the day,* or for someone else to look after him while you are at work. He needs to be fed four times a day and taken out to his toilet area after each meal, on waking, and at very frequent intervals in-between. He also needs to be accustomed gradually to spending longer periods of time alone. He does not need walks, but he does need to be taken on lots of outings to ensure he is properly socialised. His vaccinations will not yet protect him, so keep him off the ground and away from unvaccinated dogs.

From 10–12 weeks of age: Your puppy's bladder capacity is increasing but, if you go back to work, he may still be unable to last the four hours until you come home at lunch time, or until someone else comes in to see to him. If you crate him, you'll need to arrange for someone to come in and let him out *mid-morning* as well as later in the day, and he still needs four meals a day. If he has to be left alone for four hours, you'll need a large, purpose-built puppy pen to keep him safe and out of mischief. Puppies this age are best kept off your carpets. He still needs lots of socialisation outings, but no formal exercise.

From 3–6 months of age: By the time he is six months old, your puppy will probably be able to last three to four hours without a wee, and he may be happy to sleep those four hours away in a large, adult-sized crate. He will need a midday meal until he is six months old. If you are going to leave your dog for any more than four hours, he really would be better off with a puppy-pen arrangement. Bear in mind, also, that this is the age at which some dogs become very destructive, especially if they are bored. So you probably will not want to give him the run of the house while you are not there. During this period, however, you can begin to give him increasing access to carpeted areas of your home, under close supervision to begin with. By six months, you will be able to relax a little in this respect.

Give yourself a break!

Aligning your expectations with reality is the key to enjoying a puppy. Puppies are hard work. House-training takes weeks, not days. Puppies eat everything they can fit in their mouths, bite like crocodiles and growl like tigers. And puppies don't listen to anything anyone says.

This is all normal. Try to resist the temptation to turn your entire home into puppy world. Use barriers to restrict him to certain parts of the house, and allow yourself a break from him every now and then. There is a fantastic support network on the Labrador Forum for frazzled new puppy parents, so do join and make use of it (links at the back of this book). You'll soon be through this phase and ready to start having fun with your grown-up dog. In the meantime, if any aspect of your puppy's behaviour is worrying you, the next chapter is just for you.

6

Coping with puppy problems

In the last chapter, we looked at the kinds of behaviours we can expect in a new puppy, and at how to house train and socialise your new friend so that he grows up clean and friendly. Theory and principles are all very well, but what happens when things don't go according to plan? What do you do when house-training seems to be going backwards rather than forwards, and when your puppy's biting and naughtiness is getting out of hand?

Some puppies are very easy to deal with. Others can be more challenging. In this chapter, we're going to look at how to cope with some of those puppy problems that can make life less fun if not managed appropriately.

Biting and overexcitement

All puppies bite. Labrador puppies bite a lot, and very hard. Almost every week, I hear from worried puppy owners who think their puppy's biting is abnormal, or are worried that he must be becoming aggressive. The ferocious snarling that accompanies all this biting is partly what concerns people – it is perfectly normal, and only temporary. Part of the problem is the way in which we play with our puppies. For example, if you place your hand on a puppy's tummy and rub it,

This adorable face hides some very sharp teeth!

many puppies will wrap their legs around your hand and attack it. The answer is to stop rubbing your puppy's tummy in this way. This doesn't mean you won't be able to give him tummy rubs when he is older; it's just a temporary thing.

If your puppy hurts you, immediately stop any game you are having together and stand up. Some puppies will back off if you squeal with pain, but many will just come back for more. Put some space between you and the puppy so that he comes to associate biting with loss of play. If your puppy was sitting on your lap, put him on the floor. If he is biting your socks, step over a baby gate, so he cannot reach you.

A puppy bite may occasionally draw blood, but it is not the crushing bite that puppies use to crack through bones and tear up meat, even though it might feel that way at times! It is a play-bite, even though it hurts. Eventually, we want our puppies never to bite at all, even in play, but this is a process. Your puppy has already learned not to harm his mother and his siblings, but their skin is covered with fur. Yours is not, and your puppy needs to learn to use his mouth softly. Don't be tempted to punish the puppy for biting, and ignore anyone who tells you to hit him, or bite him back. Physical retribution only teaches him that you are unkind, and it won't stop him biting other people. Puppies bite much harder when they are overexcited, so your priority is to behave in a way that does not encourage overexcitement and rough play between humans and dogs.

Give your puppy lots of opportunity to bite and play with toys. Rope toys are good for biting and chasing. Strong rawhide chews can help relieve the discomfort of teething, but keep hold of one end, and remove the chew if bits start to break off it. Don't let small children play rough games with puppies – they don't have the skills required to break off the game and will get the puppy so excited that his brain will melt.

Crying and barking

New puppies will cry if left alone when you first bring them home. This is a normal reaction to being abandoned in a strange place. Once your puppy has begun to settle in and accept that your home is his home, this fear should subside, and he should be happy to be left alone for short periods while you leave the room or even the house. However, some puppies get into the habit of crying and howling whenever they are left. Puppies are smart and the howling puppy has learned that if he yells loudly enough and for long enough, someone will come and reward him with their company.

This kind of howling for attention can very quickly escalate so that the puppy is now genuinely distressed. One way to avoid this problem is to leave the puppy alone many times during the early weeks, but only for very short periods of time, and to make sure that those alone times are pleasant for him by giving him a previously frozen-food-filled kong to chew on. Howling problems are much more likely if a puppy is left for too long and then released or comforted while the howling is in progress. If you already have a crying problem on your hands, you'll need to treat it with the 'click-for-quiet' approach, set out below.

Barking with excitement or frustration can become a habit, too, especially if reinforced with rewards. It is important to recognise that you do lots of things that your puppy finds rewarding, from fetching his dinner bowl to putting on your coat or picking up your car keys. If your actions predict something he likes, he will be excited, and if the thing he wants is delayed in any way at all, he will become frustrated. Some dogs will respond to excitement or frustration by barking.

The first way to tackle this is to avoid frustrating delays where possible. You can, for example, prepare your puppy's food when he is out of earshot. The second is to ignore any barking completely and consistently to avoid reinforcing it with rewards. If your puppy barks because he sees you taking his lead off its hook, do not respond by clipping it on. Wait until he is calm. If he barks as you move towards the door, don't open the door. Make going through the door contingent on your puppy being quiet.

In the intial stages of retraining, this can take a long time, so don't start this kind of behaviour modification when you need to get off to work. Do it at the weekend or when you are on holiday. Once your puppy has grasped that he has to be quiet to get what he wants, progress is rapid.

Click for quiet

I recommend you buy a clicker, an item of equipment that is cheap, convenient to carry around with you and makes a distinctive and consistent sound. The click-for-quiet technique is a way of teaching a puppy to wait quietly in his crate, even if you go out of sight. The noisiest puppy stops crying or howling momentarily. The principle of the technique is to reward the puppy each time he falls silent for a second or two, and then gradually extend those periods of silence. The reward for silence can be food, release from confinement or simply your presence. The purpose of the click is to identify the brief period of silence so that the dog knows what he is being rewarded for.

You make a click when the puppy falls silent and follow it with his reward. It doesn't matter if he has started crying again when you give him the reward because the click identifies for the puppy the behaviour that is being rewarded.

Let's say you want your puppy to rest quietly in his crate for half an hour while you relax in another room, but as soon as you leave the room, the puppy starts whining. Have your clicker in your hand and wait out of sight for the puppy to pause. Click as soon as he falls silent, return to him and get him out of the crate for a brief cuddle. Now place him straight back in his crate and leave the room. Off he'll go again with his whining or howling. Keep repeating, and before long, he'll fall silent almost immediately you have left him or even not start crying at all. He is beginning to realise that silence earns your return. Now you can start to extend the time you leave him for. Over the next few hours and days, you'll be able to build up to two or three minutes, and from there, it is only a matter of time before he will sit quietly for the entire half-hour that you originally wanted.

It is a natural response to avoid doing the thing that upsets your puppy, but this makes it even more upsetting in the long run. If you avoid leaving your puppy alone, he never gets any opportunity to learn that being alone for a short while won't hurt him. By leaving your puppy very frequently and rewarding him for waiting quietly, he has plenty of opportunity to discover that life goes on, nothing bad happens, and that being alone for a little while is okay.

Destructive behaviour

Most people realise that puppies chew things, and they provide puppies with their own toys to teeth on. Unfortunately, many hard toys, which look ideal for chewing, are relatively unattractive to puppies, who much prefer to gnaw on your slippers or rip up the nice cuddly toys you bought for them to carry around.

Very few chew toys are actually dog proof, so you will need to keep an eye on them and replace them when bits start to come off. Some chew toys need careful supervision. These include large, knotted-rope toys and rawhide. Most puppies love rawhide chews, but will quickly disassemble them if left to their own devices. Rawhide can be used, but buy bigger chews than you think you will need, and supervise the puppy closely, removing the chew as soon as he starts to work it loose or break bits off. Apart from the risk of choking on small lumps, if he swallows the bits, and he will, he is likely to vomit the whole lot up later while you are trying to enjoy your supper.

By far and away the best chew toy is the puppy kong, but your puppy won't be terribly impressed with it unless you play your part. The secret to puppy joy is the hollow centre, which you should fill with softish puppy food and then freeze. When you need to redirect the puppy away from your chairlegs, the frozen kong will provide him with a substantial period of entertainment. You'll need three or four so that there is always one ready in the freezer. And it is a great idea to leave him with one each time you go out without him, so that he associates you leaving with a great treat.

No matter how clever you are with your frozen kong supply and your supervised rope and rawhide toys, your Labrador puppy will probably still want to chew your stuff. Leaving a puppy alone in any part of your house where you have precious items is a big mistake. This is just one more reason to confine your young puppy to a small part of your house to begin with. This gives you a much smaller area to puppy proof and in which to nag at the family to pick up their things.

In the garden, chewing up plants can be a problem. Some puppies are also surprisingly good at digging and will excavate substantial holes in your lawn or vegetable patch if left alone for very long. Others have a preference for emptying tubs and planters. If you don't want to spend all your spare time on puppy-watch, your best bet is to provide a dedicated, puppy-proof area where he can play outdoors when the weather is fine.

Everything goes in her mouth - young Labradors love to chew.

Tummy troubles and eating rubbish

Upset tummies are a common problem in puppies. Moving home at eight weeks old is quite an upheaval for such a very young animal, and this can often set off a bout of diarrhoea, as can big meals, or a change in diet. The best way to keep your puppy's digestion in nice working order is to introduce any changes in his life as gradually as possible, and to avoid too many different changes at once. In other words, try not to pile on the stress. If your puppy has persistent diarrhoea or is vomiting, he really needs to see a vet straightaway. Don't wait until after the weekend. Puppies can get dehydrated very quickly, and the symptoms may indicate an infection that needs treating.

Some puppies seem to be on a mission to chew or swallow things that upset them. Like babies, puppies love to explore the world with their mouths. They pick up and chew all kinds of things, from twigs and stones to bits of paper and anything small you leave lying around, such as coins, batteries or bottle tops. Sometimes they swallow these things, but mostly they just chew on them for a while, roll them around in their mouths and, if left alone, eventually spit them out. When you know your puppy has something potentially dangerous in his mouth, the temptation is to rush over, grab him, stick your fingers in his mouth and remove the offending item. This may work a time or two; then the puppy will wise up, and next time you approach, he will put the item where you can't get it – in his stomach.

The best approach when you see your puppy with something scary in his mouth is to *head straight for the fridge* and grab something delicious to eat. I appreciate that this is not a suitable time to stop for a snack, but the food is for the puppy not for you! Hold up a nice lump of cheese, make yummy appreciative noises and wave it around where the puppy can clearly see it. Don't try to grab him; just show him the food. Nine times out of ten, the puppy will spit out the coin he was contemplating swallowing, and run over to get the treat.

Next time he puts something inappropriate in his mouth, he'll be less likely to swallow it if you approach him. If the worst comes to the worst and your puppy succeeds in swallowing something you think may harm him, phone your veterinary surgery for advice.

Guarding and possessiveness

Labrador puppies love to pick things up in their mouths and run around with them – *your* things. Just as when he is chewing on something potentially dangerous, the best way to get your puppy to release your favourite scarf or heartbreakingly expensive best shoes, is to swap for something the puppy wants more. Food is usually your best bet, although some puppies will sell their souls for a favourite toy. Never get involved in an unseemly tussle with your puppy over something he wants, or chase him when he is carrying something you want. All this teaches him is a) you are mean, and b) running away from you is fun.

Food is a great swap item for most puppies, but what happens when the puppy is being possessive over food itself? What should you do when the puppy growls at you when he is eating his dinner, or when you go to take an old chew toy from him? In the old days, puppies that growled would be physically punished. Nowadays, we know that this can cause serious aggression problems. Punishment for growling does two things: it teaches the puppy not to growl when he feels threatened; and it sometimes (if harsh enough) teaches the puppy to fear the person dishing out the punishment. Unfortunately, it doesn't teach the puppy not to guard stuff from people who have never punished him, which includes most of the human race. And even more seriously, punishment for growling removes your dog's vital early-warning system. Growling lets you know that the dog feels very threatened and that he may be prepared to bite if you keep pushing him. Stopping the growling does not stop aggression, it just removes your safety net; nor does it reduce the risk of a bite. Punishment-based treatment of growling and guarding is a very dangerous and ineffective way to make dogs safe around people, so please don't be tempted to use it on your Labrador or to let anyone else do this to your dog.

Growling over food is extremely common in puppies and does not mean your puppy is inherently aggressive. It simply means he is worried you will take his food away. Treatment for growling in puppies is simple, and involves convincing the puppy that people coming near his food is a really good thing. This usually takes just a few days.

The first step is to establish a baseline, a distance between you and the puppy's food bowl that he feels comfortable with. Watch his body language. You are waiting not only for the growling to stop, but also for the puppy to relax. If he stiffens or freezes, you are too close. Back off a little until your puppy can relax, and from here, throw little tasty treats near or around your dog's bowl. Do this each time you feed him. Put his bowl on the floor, back off and throw some tasty bits of roast meat or tiny cubes of cheese around his bowl. Each meal time, you will be able to get a little closer to the puppy as he realises that you are just there to make mealtimes even better. Soon, you'll be able to touch him while he is eating. Back off if he feels threatened at any point.

Once he is happy to be touched gently, you can stroke and pet him more vigorously and gradually put your hands closer to his bowl when you add the tasty treats. Eventually, you'll be able to lift the bowl a few inches off the floor to add some treats. Never take the bowl away from the puppy unless he is completely happy about it, and whenever you remove food from a puppy, always return it with something better in the bowl. He'll soon trust you completely around food, and you can repeat this process by getting other people to do the same as you have just done. This will make sure your puppy grows up to be safe around people while he is eating.

House-training issues

Everyone knows that small puppies need to be house-trained, but it can be frustrating when things don't go as expected. Let's look at a few common problems.

Puppies that won't wee outdoors

If your puppy won't wee outdoors, you need to play a waiting game. Many people don't realise that they need to supervise their puppy at his outside toilet area to begin with. If you let him out on his own, the chances are he'll just wait by the door for you to let him in again. Go outside with him, and wait with him, until he has emptied his bladder. This is more fun in summer, but it has to be done in winter, too. So if the weather is poor, get yourself properly kitted out with some warm clothes before going into the garden with your puppy. A chair in the garden and a book to read can help pass the time. Your best chance of a result is after your puppy has eaten a meal, woken from a nap or had a really exciting game.

Weeing indoors after toileting outdoors

People often tell me that their puppy empties his bladder outside, then comes indoors and ten minutes later there is a puddle on the kitchen floor. Where does it all come from? And why is he not waiting, or asking to go out? This is a temporary but very common problem. Small puppies have very little control over their bladders to begin with and some puppies need to be taken outside very frequently – even at twenty-minute intervals – at certain times of the day, during the first week or so. If your puppy is like this, it may or may not help to give him access to the garden via an open door for a few days. Some pups just don't want to be outside alone to begin with. This very frequent need to toilet is one of the reasons why you really do need someone to be with a small puppy for much of the day. This phase soon passes if you focus on making sure that you help your puppy reach the right place to toilet every time, so that he doesn't get into the habit of toileting indoors.

Not asking to go out

'Why doesn't my puppy ask to go out?' is a common question. Many small puppies wait quietly by the kitchen door and if no one notices them, they will be forced to empty themselves where they are. Don't expect your Labrador puppy to whine or bark in order to be let out. Very few Labradors do this, and those that do can end up making a nuisance of themselves by fussing to be let out when it isn't convenient for you. It's your job to ensure that your puppy is let out at appropriate intervals, not his to remind you.

Going backwards with house-training

It can be very disappointing to think that you have won the whole house-training battle, only to find that your puppy has taken a huge step backwards and is messing in the house all over again. If your puppy is ten weeks old and clean, it is tempting to conclude that he is house-trained. The reality is that he isn't house-trained yet. What has happened is that you have done, and are doing, a brilliant job of helping him get to his toilet area when he needs to, and of supervising him in-between visits to the garden. After a couple of weeks of this intensive effort, it is only human for you to let standards slide a little. Many people start spacing their garden trips too far apart at this point, or letting their puppy have access to carpets, or just failing to watch him very closely, with the inevitable puddles and parcels on the floor. Don't panic if this happens to you. You haven't messed up, and your puppy isn't a failure. Just take a step back and supervise your puppy more closely for a while, with more frequent trips to the garden.

Bedwetting

Bedwetting is another problem that some people ask me about. Again, this is a question of handler error rather than anything to do with the puppy. All puppies are born with a natural instinct to keep their bed clean. So they won't wee in their bed if they can possibly help it, but if trapped there, once their bladder is full, the puppy will be forced to wet himself. If your puppy is sleeping through the night in a small crate, do feel his blankets in the morning to make sure you did not leave him too long. If he wets the bed a few times, he *will* stop minding, and he will stop trying to keep himself clean. If your puppy is able to leave his bed and is wetting it, or starts wetting it after being clean for *several months*, he needs to be checked by a vet to make sure he hasn't picked up a urinary tract infection.

Submissive urination

If your puppy greets visitors by urinating at (or on) their feet, don't panic! This is common puppy behaviour and will be outgrown as your puppy gains in confidence. Like all aspects of house-training, time and patience wins the day, and this challenging few weeks will soon be a distant memory.

SUMMARY

Getting into conflict with a small puppy is a really bad idea. Remember that biting is normal between littermates, and between puppies and older dogs. Play-biting teaches puppies how hard they can bite without hurting, but dogs have fur coats to protect them, and it takes time for a puppy to learn how delicate human skin is. Puppies also growl, sometimes quite savagely, pull at your clothes, bark, cry and pee on the floor long after you think they should have stopped.

All this is completely normal. House-training is often one step forwards and two steps back. Many people still say to me that they are worried their tiny puppy is attempting to become dominant over them, or is being disobedient, when he appears to defy their wishes or is getting too rough. This, too, is all perfectly normal and has nothing whatever to do with dominance or pack leadership. We'll look at that in a bit more detail later in this book, but rest assured, your Labrador puppy has absolutely no desire whatsoever to be in charge. He just wants to have fun.

One of your key priorities as your puppy grows up will be to keep him fit and well. In the next two chapters, we'll be dealing with various aspects of caring for a Labrador on a day-to-day basis, beginning with health.

Puppies just want to have fun!

7

Your Labrador's health

Whether or not your Labrador is blessed with good health will depend on a combination of factors that influence him both before and after his birth. These factors include the genes that your dog has inherited from his parents, and the environment he is exposed to as he is growing up. That's where your influence is most important.

Many people worry about their dog's health – when or whether to take him to the vet, whether or not to vaccinate him, how much to feed him, what to do if he gets sick or has an accident. We'll be taking a look at these concerns and giving you some guidelines to put your mind at rest. The cost of modern veterinary treatment is another important issue, so before we go any further, let's talk about whether or not you should insure your dog.

Vets and insurance

A veterinary surgeon is not just a general practitioner for animals; he/she is also a qualified surgeon with access to a well-equipped, modern operating theatre and the latest in diagnostic equipment and medical treatments. Modern medical treatment of any sort can be extremely expensive and your pet's veterinary care is no exception. Any kind of operation will cost you an arm and a leg as you will be responsible for X-rays, anaesthetics, blood tests, drugs, your vet's time and that of the nursing team. Treatment for a long-term illness can be cripplingly expensive since many modern drugs are costly.

If you don't want to find yourself choosing between your annual holiday and your pet's life, I strongly recommend that you consider taking out a veterinary-insurance policy that won't cut you off the following year if the dog develops a long-term condition, such as hip dysplasia or cancer. Check the small print carefully. Cheaper policies are not always the bargain they at first appear to be.

Veterinary insurance is expensive, and if you have several dogs, you may want to consider setting up a savings fund for them instead. Either way, it is important to have some money set aside somewhere to pay up if your dog gets sick.

Vaccinations

Your new puppy will need a course of vaccinations to protect him from a number of diseases that have not yet been eradicated from the domestic dog population. Check with your vet which vaccinations apply. It varies from one country to another. At one time, annual vaccinations were the norm, but the World Small Animal Veterinary Association now recommends a three-year gap for some core vaccinations, and annual intervals for others. Many new dog owners are worried about dangers of vaccination and of *over*vaccinating, and it is true that all vaccines carry a risk of side effects. However, studies have shown this to be very small, whereas the risk of your puppy dying if he contracts parvovirus, for example, is very high. There are no known *effective* alternatives to mainstream vaccinations, so it really does make sense to vaccinate your small puppy.

Labrador puppies are heavy to carry around, and because socialisation is so important, it is tempting to try to get your puppy vaccinated early. Some breeders do give their puppies their first vaccination before they go to their new homes, but many vets warn against this practice, partly because puppies still have maternal antibodies at this age, and these antibodies interfere with the vaccine. Another reason is that your vet may use a different brand of vaccine from your breeder's vet, which means starting the course all over again when you get your puppy home.

Your puppy will probably need two or three shots to achieve immunity (depending on your vet and the diseases in your local area). These will usually be spaced a few weeks apart, and your vet will tell you that it will be a few weeks *after* the last shot before your puppy can run around safely on contaminated ground or play safely with unvaccinated dogs. Many people are able to join a puppy playgroup after first vaccinations have been given, and this enables puppies to socialise with other vaccinated pups. In public locations, you'll find it helpful to have a strong shoulder bag in which to carry your puppy around.

Once your puppy has completed his initial course of vaccinations, your vet will ask to see him at yearly intervals for a check-up and booster. If you are concerned about overvaccination, you can pay for a blood test, called a titre, to see if your puppy still has immunity from the last one. This may give you the option to delay vaccination if you wish. Vaccination is often a contentious topic, but the reason most puppies, even very young unvaccinated puppies, are usually able to be taken out and about safely is because we have high levels of immunity in the general domestic dog population. The reason this herd immunity exists is because the people all around us are vaccinating their dogs. Giving your dog immunity not only protects him, it protects your neighbours' and friends' puppies, too.

Parasite control

Domestic dogs are prone to a range of internal and external parasites. They can get roundworms in their heart, lungs and intestines, and, as adults, they are very prone to intestinal tapeworms. Your puppy should have been treated for roundworms every two weeks since birth. Your vet will supply safe and effective wormers for your dog and repeat supplies can often be purchased online.

You may have read that natural wormers are better for dogs, but there is no evidence to support this view. Wormers supplied by your vet have been proven to work and are tolerated very well by most dogs. It is worth remembering that intestinal roundworms carried by puppies can and do infect people, especially children, and can cause serious illness. There are laboratories that, for a fee, will test a sample of your dog's faeces. You can use this system to check for intestinal worms in your older dog if you want to reduce the amount of wormers you use in the long term.

External parasites are also common and can be treated as and when necessary. Fleas often make their presence felt by biting the ankles of human family members, and dogs will react to an infestation by nibbling the base of their tail and frequent scratching. Chemical treatments will deal with the infestation on your dog, but you may also need to vacuum very thoroughly indeed for a while, and possibly treat your carpets, to get rid of them entirely. Some canine flea treatments are very toxic to cats, so if you have a cat, be careful what you use to treat your dog. A whole range of flea treatments are available, some of which have to be applied to your dog's skin, and some of which have to be swallowed. Talk to your vet about which is most suited to your dog – different products may cover a different combination of parasites, and where you live needs to be considered.

In some areas, ticks are a problem. These are tiny creatures that attach themselves to your dog's skin and swell to the size of a small bean as they feed on his blood. The main problem with ticks is that they may carry Lyme disease, which can have serious, even life-threatening, consequences for both people and dogs. If you live in a Lyme-disease area, it is important to use a preventative tick treatment, such as one of the spot-on chemicals. In other areas, you might be able to rely on simply checking for ticks and removing any you find attached to your dog at the end of each walk. You can purchase tick-remover tools very cheaply online. Never try to burn a tick or suffocate it with oil or detergent to make it drop off because this may make it regurgitate its stomach contents into your dog and increase the risk of infection.

Ear mites are another common parasite and an infestation can make your Labrador quite miserable. The symptoms are shaking the head vigorously, so that the ears flap, and pawing at the ears with the front feet. Diagnosis needs to be made by your vet, because other problems can also cause these symptoms. The treatment for ear mites is usually straightforward. Your vet will confirm the diagnosis and prescribe a course of treatment.

Probably the single biggest health problem affecting domestic Labradors today is an excess of body fat, and this is one area where you can achieve a great result with some commitment and care.

Diet and exercise are key factors in your Labrador's health.

Preventing and treating obesity

Many vets claim that the majority of Labradors they see now are overweight. This is a real tragedy because obesity increases the risk of a number of disorders, puts strain on your dog's joints and organs, and generally reduces the quality and length of his life. It is also entirely avoidable, because although Labradors are greedy dogs, there is no need for any Labrador to have any say in how much or how often he eats. Despite this, many Labrador owners really struggle to keep their dogs slim. Often, this is because they are guessing at quantities instead of measuring food, and feeding snacks to the dog in between mealtimes.

People with fat dogs often tell me they walk miles with the dog every day, and I believe them. The problem is that dogs, like people, are efficient converters of energy, and they can run a very long way on quite a small amount of food. Of course, your Labrador needs his daily walks, but the key to controlling your dog's waistline is less food. In addition, if your dog is already very overweight, increasing his exercise too quickly may put an added strain on his system.

Sadly, we are so used to seeing overweight Labradors that many people actually worry their dog is too thin when he is genuinely too fat. You don't need to weigh your dog to know whether or not he is fat. Simply run your hands along his flank and feel for his ribs. If you cannot easily feel them, he is probably overweight. Now look at him from the side. Does his belly slope up towards his loins? If not, he is probably overweight. Look at him from above. Do his sides curve in to form a waist before his hips? If not, he is probably overweight.

You don't need special food or instructions to slim down your dog. You just need to reduce his food by one third. Pour his normal ration of food into a bowl, then tip the contents into your scales. Make a note of how much his meal weighed and calculate what two-thirds of that quantity would be. That is his daily ration from now on. If you don't want to weigh his food every day, use a measuring cup or container that holds just the right amount, or mark the side with the new quantity. Now feed your dog this reduced quantity of food every day for a week and re-assess his condition. No change? Reduce the quantity a little more, re-assessing your dog at weekly intervals. Make sure all other members of the family understand why you are doing this, and how important it is for your dog's health. If they want to use food for training or as a treat, it needs to come out of this daily allowance. Nothing else should be given to the dog.

Provided your dog is not ill, absolutely no harm will come to him if you reduce his rations in this way for a week. If he pesters you for more food, take him outside and throw a ball for him instead. If you are worried that he is not getting enough

Retrieving games are a great way to stay active and keep slim.

enjoyment from his meals, put them in a slow-food bowl or a treat dispenser to string the meal out for a bit longer. If you get disheartened or feel sorry for him, just remind yourself you may well be saving his life. Thousands of people have slimmed down their dogs like this, and you can, too.

Accidents and emergencies

We all hope that our dog will never have a serious accident, but we can do better than hope. The risk of accidents can be greatly reduced by following some basic precautions. Securing the perimeter of your property so that your dog can never leave it without you is the first and foremost way to prevent accidents. When I was small, many dogs were allowed to wander freely in the community, but nowadays, there are simply too many hazards. Training a reliable recall response and always keeping a dog leashed in areas where there is access to traffic, no matter how well behaved he may be, also goes a long way towards ensuring your dog's safety.

Safety around water

It's worth remembering that traffic isn't the only hazard. We have an extensive network of coastal paths in the UK, but these are not always safe places to walk with an off-lead Labrador. Every year, dogs fall over cliffs and have to be rescued. Some are fatally injured.

Taking care around water is important in both summer and winter. No matter how good a swimmer your dog is, a lifejacket is a sensible precaution if you take him boating. As well as the added buoyancy, it is much easier to haul a slippery, tired dog back into a boat if he is wearing something you can grasp easily. In winter, ice can be a serious hazard for the water-loving dog, so do keep your dog leashed around rivers and ponds when the surface is frozen.

Heatstroke

It isn't a good idea to take your dog with you to the beach on a hot summer's day. Dogs lose a lot of water from their bodies when they pant. So, even if you have plenty of shade and your dog can be persuaded to stay in it, he needs *constant* access to plenty of fresh water in hot weather. Labradors are tough dogs but running or sunbathing with your dog in high temperatures is very risky. The symptoms of heatstroke are not always easy to spot until the dog actually becomes distressed or collapses, but excessive panting and drooling are often your first warning signs.

Don't forget that dogs should never be left alone in a car in warm temperatures, not even for a few minutes – you could have an accident and be unable to return – and not even with the windows open a crack. The temperature inside a metal vehicle rises dangerously within just a few minutes of being parked in sunshine. The nice shady spot you found won't still be shady once the sun has moved around a bit. To be cooked alive is a terrible fate and you would never forgive yourself if it happened to your dog. Finally, don't forget that dogs can overheat indoors, too, so don't leave a dog trapped in a room dominated by a large sunny window.

The treatment for heatstroke is to remove the dog from the heat source, and immediately start to cool him down with cool (*not* freezing cold) water. You could also place a bag of frozen peas on the back of his neck, and massaging his legs will help. Stop cooling the dog once his temperature falls below about 39°C (103°F) and get him to a vet. You can take your dog's temperature by carefully inserting a thermometer a short way into his rectum. Ask your vet to show you how, and don't forget to store the thermometer separately from the ones you use for humans!

Bloat

Bloat occurs when the dog's stomach becomes dangerously distended. When this happens, the stomach may rotate, cutting off its own blood supply. Bloat is more common in larger, deep-chested dogs, and in dogs with a close relative that has suffered from this condition. It is a potentially fatal medical emergency.

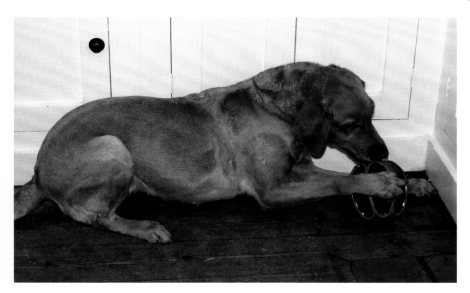

Treat dispensers can slow down fast eaters.

Many Labrador owners worry about this horrible condition and want to know how they can avoid it happening to their own dog. The causes of bloat, and why some dogs are more susceptible to it than others, are not precisely known, although there is clearly a genetic element. Studies into bloat have found a variety of risk factors, including:

- A large volume of food consumed in a single sitting.
- Having a close relative that has suffered from bloat.
- Rapid consumption of food.
- Eating from raised bowls.
- A diet restricted to certain types of dry food.

Labradors love food and are often very fast eaters. If you are concerned about your dog bolting his food, you can buy a slow-feed bowl, or treat dispensers, which prevent him from eating large quantities of kibble at speed.

Symptoms of bloat are a hard, swollen stomach that is clearly making the dog uncomfortable. He may try to be sick but be unable to bring anything up. In some dogs, symptoms may be less obvious. If you are worried that your dog might have bloat, speed is of the essence. If it happens late in the evening, don't be tempted to wait until morning, because he may not survive the night. Phone your vet to let him know you are on your way and leave immediately. The faster the dog is treated, the less the internal damage will be.

Cuts and broken bones

Sometimes dogs have accidents or get into fights. Before you can help an injured dog, yours or anyone else's, you must ensure your own safety. Dogs in pain may bite, no matter how wonderful their temperament. Biting is an instinctive canine reaction to severe pain. If you need to muzzle a dog in order to help him, do so. A scarf tied gently around his muzzle may be sufficient. A coat or towel over his head may help to keep him calm, while you assess the situation. If your dog is bleeding profusely, you must put pressure on the wound. Ideally, make a pad out of a piece of clothing and press firmly onto the cut while you get veterinary advice. Puncture wounds from fights may look small but they can be deep and may become infected. If your dog is involved in a fight, let your vet give him a good check over.

In the unlikely event that your dog is ever involved in a serious accident, a good knowledge of first aid might save his life. Some veterinary practices run first-aid courses for dog owners. These are a great idea if you can find one near you. It is much easier to administer first aid if you have been given practical demonstrations and hands-on advice. Hopefully, you'll never need the skills you learn.

Common ailments

It is sometimes difficult to know what is normal, what requires a routine vet's appointment and what is an emergency. It isn't possible for me to give you an exhaustive list of all the ailments that your dog might suffer from, and a book is not really the appropriate place to seek medical help. However, a few ailments are very common and worth discussing here, if only so that you know what to look for and when to get help.

Tummy troubles

Digestive problems are probably one of the most common causes of concern. Diarrhoea or vomiting can be a symptom of a range of health problems, but may not necessitate an immediate visit to the vet. It is not unusual for a dog to bring back his dinner immediately after eating, and then consume it again. This is normal, if a little gross. A single episode of diarrhoea is nothing to worry about, provided the dog's stools return to normal within a few hours. However, a healthy dog should not be repeatedly vomiting or retching or having repeated bouts of diarrhoea. These symptoms require veterinary attention. Small puppies are especially vulnerable to dehydration and need a same-day veterinary check if they are suffering from diarrhoea and vomiting.

Ear troubles

Ear problems are not uncommon in floppy-eared dogs, and Labradors are no exception. The flap covers the entrance to the ear canal and creates a moist warm environment, which favours infection and parasites. The symptoms are head shaking and rubbing or pawing at the ears, and warrant an appointment to see the vet. Tipping the head on one side or loss of balance can also indicate an ear infection, but may be a sign of something more serious, so these need more urgent attention. Give your vet a ring and ask for advice. Don't let ear flapping go on for days on end or your Labrador could end up with a haematoma. This is a large, blood-filled sac inside the ear flap, which can burst at any time. The results are quite dramatic and usually require surgery to fix permanently. You'll save a lot of mess, and your wallet, if you deal with this promptly.

Skin troubles

Various types of dermatitis, often as a result of allergies, seem to be quite common in Labradors. It can be difficult to get to the bottom of what is causing skin allergies and it is well worth getting help from a specialist vet dermatologist if your vet is struggling to find a treatment that works. Sometimes it can take patience and a long course of treatment to resolve the problem. If your dog has a persistent rash, hair loss, spots or pimples or a sore area of skin, get it looked at by the vet. There are numerous possible causes, from allergies to fleas or food, to an underlying illness.

Lameness

Arthritis is common in Labradors. It may not appear until old age, but it can appear in younger dogs. It can sometimes be linked to a joint defect, such as hip or elbow dysplasia. These two conditions may require surgery to fix them and the initial symptoms are often lameness. Many other conditions cause lameness, so don't despair if your dog is limping. Do take him to the vet as soon as possible, for both pain relief and the best treatment outcome.

Don't be tempted to give your dog human painkillers – aspirin, for example, can be harmful to dogs. Dogs with arthritis can often be given a whole new lease of life by a little pain relief and some weight loss. Listen to your vet's advice on this one.

When to call the vet

Sometimes a dog will fall, be hurt or get sick and his owner will be unsure of whether or not veterinary attention is needed. Try not to overthink this, and don't hesitate to telephone your vet and describe the symptoms to him if you are not sure. Very general guidelines are:

- If your dog is limping, dragging a limb, or if a limb looks misshapen, he needs a vet.
- If he has a deep cut, is bleeding profusely, seems to be in pain and does not want you to touch part of his body that he is normally fine about having touched, he needs to see a vet.
- If he has a discharge from any part of his body, or an unexplained lump on his body, he needs to see a vet.
- If he is retching, vomiting, straining to go to the toilet without success or having diarrhoea repeatedly, he needs veterinary attention.

This is not an exclusive list, so you need to trust your own instincts. Sick dogs are sometimes very good at hiding the symptoms. If your dog seems withdrawn, reluctant to exercise, loses his appetite or becomes excessively thirsty, these are not normal behaviours. You need to talk to your vet about them.

If your gut feeling is that your dog isn't quite right, listen to it and pick up the phone. Far too many people rush to the Internet or a book for veterinary help simply because they are not sure if they need an appointment. Your vet is only a telephone call away. Most vets will happily answer questions over the phone and tell you whether or not your dog needs a routine appointment, or whether you should bring him in without delay. This is usually a free service and it's important to make use of it.

Your healthy dog

Most Labradors are fairly healthy dogs. Of course, there will be ups and down, days when his tummy is a bit upset, and there will be minor bumps and bruises. It's all part of growing up. Try not to worry overmuch about your dog's health. To a certain extent, you'll need to trust your own judgement. Get to know what is normal for him and how he behaves, looks and feels when he is well. That way, you'll rapidly spot any changes in his behaviour or appearance.

There is no better, hands-on, way to spend time with your dog than in regular daily training and grooming sessions. Paying attention to your dog's daily needs and care will help you to build a great relationship together and ensure that you will be the first to spot any problems, or changes in his health should they occur. In the next chapter, we're going to look at your dog's daily care, and at what you need to do to keep him in tip-top condition.

8

Daily care of your Labrador

We all want our dogs to be properly cared for, but what exactly does that mean? Many people who write to me want to know how to feed their dog and how much exercise he should have. They want to know if its okay to go running with a ten-month-old puppy and how often they should bath their dog or cut his nails. They also want to know how to amuse their dog when he is bored, when they can swap his crate for a basket, and many other aspects of daily life that experienced dog owners no longer think about. If you have never had a dog before, all these things can be a worry, and my aim is to set your mind at rest.

Life changes when you get a dog, and not just daily life. Annual events, such as holidays, can be more challenging to arrange. Going away is a much bigger deal than it once was. Should you take your dog with you? How do you find dog-friendly places to stay? What if you have to leave him behind? There is quite a bit to consider, so let's get straight on and look at the ins and outs of life with a Labrador. We'll start with every Labrador's favourite topic – food.

What should you feed your Labrador?

Over the last twenty years, kibble has taken over from canned dog meat as the most popular way to feed a dog. Kibble is a processed food in dehydrated pellet form. It is made from a range of protein sources, usually some meats, such as lamb and chicken, with plenty of cereal fillers, such as wheat or rice, and added vitamins and minerals. The aim is to provide a balanced diet for the modern dog. It is an incredibly convenient way to feed your Labrador and the majority of dog owners will probably choose to feed their pets this way.

In recent years, there has been a growth of interest in a very different method of feeding. You may have heard of BARF (biologically appropriate raw food). A similar system of raw feeding, RMB (the raw meaty bones diet), is the one I use. I switched to RMB because my kibble-fed dogs were suffering from dirty teeth and because I had, and still have, ready access to plenty of fresh meaty bones.

Raw feeding is becoming increasingly popular.

Feeding systems seem to cause very strong feelings, and there are quite a few myths circulating about both ways of feeding. Unfortunately, no proper studies have been done to compare the health of dogs fed on these two very different regimes, and so, for the most part, we have no way of knowing which claims are accurate, and which are not.

Some studies have shown that kibble-fed dogs are more likely to suffer from bloat, which might be a concern if your dog is at risk from this condition (if, for example, he has a close relative who suffered from bloat). The bones consumed by raw-fed dogs do have an abrasive cleansing action on teeth, but it is entirely possible for you to teach your dog to let you clean his teeth twice a day, if you prefer. Neither raw-fed nor kibble-fed dogs have a monopoly on shiny coats or general good health, and we just don't know if raw feeding reduces a dog's risk of allergies, as people have claimed; nor is there any truth in the myth that feeding raw will reduce the need for vaccination or worming. In fact, in some cases, a raw-fed dog needs worming more often, not less.

One of the disadvantages of raw feeding is in puppy training. With small puppies, it is entirely possible, and sometimes desirable, to use up their entire daily food ration in training new behaviours, teaching them to go into their crates, basic obedience and so on. This is not quite so simple with a raw-fed dog as a kibble-fed one.

So, which method is right for you? You will probably find it easier to feed a small puppy on kibble, and then, if you wish, switch over to raw when your dog is older and training is well under way. I also recommend that you don't feed raw if you have small children, because it is so difficult to make sure little kids wash their hands properly after handling dogs, and a raw-fed dog will get raw-meat juices all over his lips and paws. In addition, a dog is far more likely to guard raw food than kibble, and although this is treatable, it just gives you another problem to solve and is likely to make parents very jittery.

Feeding schedules

Puppies need feeding little and often, not necessarily because they cannot eat all their daily allowance in one go, but because if they do, it is likely to upset their tummies. This is especially important in kibble-fed dogs.

8–12 weeks old

Feed your puppy four times a day. There should be at least three hours (preferably four) between meals, and the last meal should be at least three hours before you go to bed, so that the puppy can empty himself before being left for the night. For example, 7am, 11am, 3pm and 7pm, with a last trip to the garden at 10 or 11pm, would work well for many families.

3–6 months

Three meals a day – breakfast, lunch and tea – work well for most pups of this age.

Over 6 months

If your puppy is to remain on kibble, it is a good idea to feed twice a day for the rest of his life. If he has a close relative that has suffered from bloat, you might want to consider switching to raw at this point. Raw-fed dogs can drop down to one meal a day at a year old if you wish.

Harmful foods

Certain common human foods are poisonous to dogs. They include (but are not limited to) the following everyday ingredients that you are quite likely to have around your home:

- Onions
- Grapes
- Raisins/sultanas
- Chocolate
- Chewing gum containing xylitol (a sweetener)

You will almost certainly know of a dog that has eaten one or more of these things *without* coming to harm, but that is because the effects are dependent on a number of factors, including the weight of the dog and how much he has eaten. Every veterinary hospital sees cases of chocolate poisoning around Christmas and Easter, and all these other ingredients are well documented as being dangerous for dogs, and in some cases fatal. The toxicity of chocolate also depends on how dark it is. Just because your friend's dog didn't get sick after eating a bar of chocolate, does not mean your dog will be okay.

Not actually poisonous, but very bad for your dog, is any form of sugary or sweet food. He doesn't need biscuits, cookies, sweets or cake and is totally dependent on you to make sure no one gives him this kind of food. So you'll need to be on the lookout for people who respond to those pleading eyes.

Out in the countryside, watch out in case your dog decides that he likes to eat plants, mushrooms and rubbish that he finds lying around – many dogs do. At certain times of the year, these are real risks and vulnerable dogs may need to be muzzled outdoors.

After food and exercise, sleep ranks high on a Labrador list of preferred activities, so let's take a look at providing your dog with his own space for rest and relaxation.

Sleeping arrangements and crating

Most people provide their Labrador with his own bed or basket but in many homes the dog will rarely sleep there. How you feel about bed sharing or allowing the dog on the sofa is a personal matter. Provided that your dog never attempts to guard the furniture he sleeps on, and if you don't mind the hairs, there is no reason why you shouldn't snuggle up together. If your dog grumbles when someone attempts to sit down next to him, it's time to think again.

Many young Labradors will sleep in a crate for the first year or so. This has its benefits. It can assist with house-training, and is helpful in families with small children because it gives the dog a haven where he cannot be disturbed. Perhaps the best benefit of crate sleeping is that the Labrador cannot chew through your table legs while you slumber upstairs. Once he is past the chewing stage, many people replace the crate with a basket.

Don't be in too much of a hurry to get rid of the crate. I tend to do this when my Labradors reach twelve to eighteen months of age, depending on how enthusiastic they are about chewing. This also tends to be the age at which you can indulge in a good-quality bed without your dog ripping it to shreds. If your dog sleeps in a crate, it needs to be situated carefully. If you put it too close to a radiator, or near a sunny window, the dog may get too hot. A corner of a family room, out of draughts and where he can see and hear people around him, is ideal.

Bathing and grooming

Labradors have a very forgiving coat that does not need a great deal of attention. They do, however, shed profusely at certain times of year, and will benefit immensely from the physical contact of a regular daily brushing, with extra attention to dead-hair removal during the moult. You can use a special tool for removing dead-hair – a de-shedding tool – but be careful not to overdo it, or you'll end up with bald patches on your dog. When moulting is at its peak, you will have a lot of loose hair floating about your home, and will need to vacuum more frequently to keep on top of it. People sometimes ask me if there is a pill or potion they can give to their dog to reduce shedding and I'm afraid the answer is no. The moult is part and parcel of owning a Labrador.

Grooming helps to build a bond with your Labrador.

Your Labrador's nails will wear down naturally with regular walking outdoors, but some Labradors' claws grow so quickly that they will also need trimming on a regular basis. This is especially likely if your dog is mostly exercised on soft ground. You mustn't let your dog's claws grow too long or they will make his feet sore and deform his toes. So get your dog used to having his feet handled on a regular basis, and clip them once you can hear them clacking on the floor.

What's that smell?

Labradors love to roll in horrible substances, such as fox poo, and this is a burden we Labrador owners often have to bear, with as much good humour as possible. You may be able to spot the signs and interrupt the dog before his shoulder goes down and he rubs himself in something disgusting, but much of the time it will be too late. Fortunately, the Labrador coat is very glossy and most unpleasant substances do hose off quite easily.

There is a distinctive body odour about a Labrador (and many other gundog breeds) that you will simply get used to, and I do recommend that you avoid getting into a cycle of bathing because it doesn't do the dog's coat much good at all. Another aroma you may notice is a nasty fishy smell coming from your dog's back end. This may be accompanied by scooting, when the dog drags his bottom along the floor. These symptoms may indicate that your dog's anal glands may need emptying – not a very pleasant task and one that most people prefer to leave to the vet.

Bathing, with detergent, is not usually necessary, but if your Labrador is getting a bit smelly, you can shampoo him if you really want to. Use a shampoo designed for dogs, so it won't sting his eyes, and try to avoid shampooing in winter if he enjoys swimming, because it removes the natural oils from his coat and renders him less waterproof.

Exercise

We've already looked at exercising young puppies, and we'll talk about exercising elderly dogs later in this book. For all the ages in-between, there are a range of ways to give your dog the daily exercise he needs to keep him fit and healthy. People often associate exercising the dog with going for long walks in the countryside. Just like us, dogs need to exercise in order to keep their heart and lungs fit, and their muscles and skeleton in good condition, but taking the dog for a long relaxing walk is not the only way of achieving this. There will be times when alternative exercise is more appropriate.

Explorers and hunters

Young dogs that are becoming more independent and adventurous, and dogs with recall problems, really do benefit from a structured approach to exercise. On a traditional walk, the dog's owner tends to stroll along in one direction with the dog trotting ahead. For a dog that has a tendency to run off and explore or hunt the wildlife, this is not a good idea. A better approach is a period of exercise during which the owner heads in one direction for a while, then turns around and goes back in the direction he came from until the dog has caught up and overtaken him again. Each time the dog starts to get too far ahead, the owner about turns again and heads the other way. This is what I call 'the about-turn walk' and it is a much better way to walk a dog with a poor recall or strong hunting instincts. There is a lot more information on this, on dealing with recall problems generally and on teaching a reliable recall in my book *Total Recall*.

Recall games and retrieving

A boisterous young dog can be called backwards and forwards between two people, gradually building up distance as his fitness increases. Chasing balls or Frisbees is great exercise, and retrieving games are one of the best ways to give a dog free-running exercise under controlled conditions. This kind of managed exercise is especially valuable and important if your dog has been taking a keen interest in the local wildlife while you are out hiking together.

Managed exercise helps to keep your Labrador under control.

Swimming

Swimming is great exercise and a lot of fun. We tend to assume that all Labradors love to swim, but a surprising proportion reach adulthood without ever showing any interest in it. If you spend a lot of time around water, it is a good idea to get your dog to take some swimming practice. Rest assured, he can swim, and if he fell into a river, lake or canal, he would not sink. Just like people, though, dogs get better at swimming with practice. A competent swimmer won't panic if he falls into deep water, and will be able to paddle around, preserving his energy until he finds a way out, or someone comes to his rescue.

Encouraging your dog to be comfortable in and around water is best achieved in puppyhood as part of the whole socialisation process. But if your Labrador missed out on this stage, he can be helped to overcome his initial fear or reluctance to enter the water, although for an older dog, this may take some time and patience. However, it is never too late, and if you want to have a go, you will need to desensitise your dog gently over the course of a few weeks or months.

The first step is to persuade him to splash about happily in small volumes of water. Don't be tempted to start with a trip to the ocean or a large lake. This applies to both puppies and adults. Start small. Splashing about in small puddles, padding through a shallow brook or stream, playing in a shallow paddling pool in the garden – these are all places to begin. Your dog should be comfortable in and around water before you ask him to take his feet off the ground and actually swim.

Some Labradors, especially younger ones, will be encouraged to swim by other dogs that enjoy the water, especially if they are taken out together repeatedly. However, be aware that if a dog is really scared of water, he may become even more scared when another, more boisterous dog showers and soaks him the first time he puts his paws in.

Another approach is to get in the water with your dog. If you don't have a suitable safe stretch of water near your home in which to do this, see if you can find a hydrotherapy centre for dogs. These are special indoor pools, aimed mainly at dogs recovering from injuries, but they are also great for dogs that are anxious around water.

Retrieving is great exercise in its own right. It is also my absolute favourite method of starting a dog swimming, but it has to be done gradually. Don't be tempted to throw a ball or dummy into the water for your reluctant Labrador or young puppy to fetch. Instead, teach your Labrador to cross a tiny and insignificant puddle to get at the retrieve on the far side. You can put obstacles either side of the puddle, or even create an artificial one, so that he has no option but to go through it. You can also help him by walking through it with him to begin with.

Labradors make fun companions wherever you take them.

Once he will splash happily through a puddle and back with a ball or dummy, it is time to find a tiny shallow stream. The water should reach no more than about a third of the way up his legs at the deepest point. Again, throw the ball across to land on dry ground on the far side of the stream. If he hesitates, go with him the first time or two; race him across. Be silly about it. Have fun. He will soon forget about getting his legs wet. Over time, you can move on to deeper streams. Do not ask your dog to pick up from the water yet. Throw the retrieve to the far side of a stretch of water that he cannot run around. This is also a good principle for gundog training because it lays the foundations for crossing obstacles. Before you know it, his fear will be gone and water will be a source of fun.

If your Labrador isn't interested in retrieving, it is a really good idea to teach him how to retrieve from scratch. We'll be talking about that in our advanced training chapter (Chapter 13, Advanced training, activities and sports). Most healthy adult Labradors will benefit immensely from participating in some kind of organised sport or physical activity, and you can read about the opportunities available to you. You will also find a selection of games to play with your dog in the final chapter of this book (Chapter 17, Fun games for Labradors of any age).

Holidays

For many Labrador owners, the thought of leaving their dog behind in kennels while they go on holiday is unacceptable. Fortunately, there are plenty of ways to have a holiday with your dog. Quite a few pubs and hotels welcome a well-behaved dog, and it's possible to rent holiday cottages where dogs are permitted.

If you want to holiday abroad, it is sometimes possible to take your dog with you, but you need to prepare well in advance. The advent of the Pet Passport means that dogs can now be taken from Britain to mainland Europe. You have to meet the entry requirements for each individual country and these usually include provisos that the dog must be microchipped, vaccinated against rabies and treated for tapeworm, and that you are in possession of a pet passport or veterinary certificate for your dog. Bear in mind that vaccinations must be made several weeks before travelling. If the country you are travelling to is outside the EU, further restrictions and longer waiting times may apply, so do check the requirements. The government provides useful information via its website.

If you decide to leave your dog behind and holiday without him, you'll need to make arrangements for his care while you are away. One obvious solution is to leave him with a relative or friend. This can work well if the friend genuinely likes your dog and knows him well, and especially if you are able to return the favour in some way. Another increasingly common solution is for families to employ a house-sitter. This is a person who stays in your home while you are away, looks after your pets, waters your garden and generally keeps an eye on the place. This can be an informal arrangement with a friend or colleague or you can go through a reputable agency. If a house-sitter does not appeal to you, you may need to send your dog to a boarding kennels for the duration of your holiday.

Boarding kennels

Good boarding kennels are always full at peak holiday times, so make sure you start looking several weeks, if not months, in advance. Your dog will probably need an up-to-date vaccination certificate from your vet, so make sure this is in hand well before your trip. Some kennels may be willing to accept a recent titre test (see page 73) result.

You may like the idea of your dog being walked outside the kennel grounds, but I wouldn't recommend this. I prefer to know that my dogs are secure within the kennel compound at all times. There is so much potential for things to go wrong when several dogs are taken out to a location they do not know and supervised by a person they do not know. Your dog will not come to any harm by not being walked for a week or two, provided he has access to a secure compound outdoors where he can trot around and stretch his legs. If your dog is friendly, he will be able to exercise/play with other friendly dogs.

It is a good idea to visit the kennel of your choice well in advance. Ask to be shown around and to see where your dog will sleep and be exercised, and where his food will be prepared. When you visit, think about security. Is the kennel double gated at every possible escape point? Do the staff make sure the external gate is closed before they let you in through the internal gate? This simple precaution is woefully ignored in some kennels. Don't worry too much about the décor. It doesn't matter if the paintwork is a little shabby provided that the dogs are safe, well cared for, clean and happy.

Most happy, healthy dogs adapt quite well to kennel life and don't suffer any long-lasting effects from being left for a week or two, but the whole experience may be less traumatic for your dog if he can have a sleepover at the kennel before the real thing. Instead of being left in a completely strange place for two weeks, he is then in a familiar environment with people he has met before, and confident that you will return. This will really help prepare you both for the separation. It will also give you a better feel for the way the kennel is run.

No matter how upset we feel about leaving our dogs, the fact is, most dogs have a perfectly nice time in kennels. Try not to worry, and enjoy your holiday – he will almost certainly enjoy his.

Welcome wherever he goes

Nowadays, many people see their dog as a family member. They don't want to go on holiday or day trips without him. They want to take him everywhere they go. This is much easier to achieve with a well-mannered dog that makes himself welcome in company. You will find that the more effort you put into training your Labrador, the more often he will be included in invitations to visit or stay with friends. A well-trained dog will enhance your family outings; a badly trained dog will spoil them. For your dog to be well trained, you will need to invest a few minutes each day in training, and arm yourself with the information necessary to make progress. In the next chapter, we'll be looking at the basic principles of training, so that you have all the information you need to train your dog to a high standard.

9

Principles of Labrador training

We all want a well-behaved dog. We may disagree on the details but, for the most part, we are not looking for an obedience champion. We simply want a dog that comes when we call him and sits when we tell him to – a dog that is a pleasure to be with.

The Labrador has a big reputation as an intelligent and trainable dog, so many new puppy owners are surprised at how challenging it can be to achieve these simple things. Training a dog is a whole lot easier if you have some basic skills and knowledge, and if your expectations are realistic. Animal training isn't rocket science, but it is *science*. It's about manipulating an animal's behaviour, and it is helpful to understand the rules and principles that govern this process if you are going to have an enjoyable training experience.

Reading this chapter will give you the information you need to complete successfully the practical steps in the next one. It will help to make sure you don't get into difficulties as you train your dog, and ensure that you are able to create your own training plans for teaching skills that are not covered in this book.

Put your trainer's hat on

For the next few months, you need to become a dog trainer. This is the first principle of dog training: we are all different. What I want from a dog is not what you want from yours, or what your neighbour wants from his. Each dog is different, too. Some need help to overcome issues such as excitability or nervousness. Some need extra help in learning self-control, not to grab, pull, barge and so on.

Working your way through a series of training exercises in isolation won't equip you to deal with the myriad of problems that will arise on your training journey. You will probably be able to get your dog to sit, give paw and come when you call him *in your house* but basic training exercises won't help you to get your dog to come back when he has found another dog to play with, or is halfway across a muddy field. They won't teach you how to keep your dog walking on a loose lead when he sees a cat on the other side of the road, or when he knows that the entrance to his favourite park is just around the corner.

What you need is some basic behavioural knowledge, some basic training skills and some practical experience. That means reading through this chapter and putting your dog trainer's hat on for a while. You needn't worry about it. No special talents are required to be a dog trainer. The entry requirements are simply a willingness to learn, and a dog to practise on.

Why dogs do the things they do

Just like people, dogs have evolved to make the most of their environment. We all repeat actions that benefitted us in the past. Dogs do what benefits them. This is your second principle of dog training, and a fundamental principle of all animal behaviour. Your task is to control the consequences of your Labrador's behaviour today so as to improve his behaviour tomorrow. It isn't difficult once you know how.

There are two types of consequence you can apply to your dog's behaviour. One is punishment, the other is reinforcement. Punishment weakens behaviour, because the dog doesn't want a repeat performance, and reinforcement strengthens it. The tools we use to apply punishment are called 'aversives' and the tools we use to apply reinforcement are called 'rewards'.

These terms can cause confusion. Some people think of punishment as harsh treatment, whereas in behavioural terms, it's just something that diminishes behaviour. A lot of the punishment traditionally used in dog training is what we might call intimidation. It can be as mild as a tone of voice, a threatening body posture or facial expression. Many Labradors, especially those from working lines, are very sensitive to this kind of behaviour on the part of their owners.

Increasingly, though, there is a move away from the use of punishment and towards the use of reinforcement in dog training. We apply rewards, often in the form of food, games or opportunities to indulge in pleasurable activities, to behaviours that we like in our dogs, so that the dog is encouraged to repeat that behaviour in the future. There are a number of reasons for this change in approach. Dogs, and our friendship with them, are increasingly valued in society. Social trends are moving away from the use of pain or fear in training generally, both for animals and for children. There are also some downsides to training with punishment. It can damage the bond between dog and handler and has recently been shown to be associated with a measurable increase in aggression in dogs, even when the punishment used has been mild.

Dog training has advanced considerably in the last few years, and we have a wide range of techniques that were not available a few decades ago. As a result, dog trainers have been able, in many cases, to abandon the use of punishment altogether. This is good news for dogs and good news for their owners because it makes training a lot more pleasant. Of course, if we are going to use reinforcement as our primary training tool, we need to know how to motivate our dogs.

Motivating your dog

One of the reasons why traditional dog training relied so heavily on punishment was due to a misunderstanding about what dogs find rewarding. Many trainers relied solely on verbal praise as a reward, and some used a combination of praise and petting. Recent studies have shown that verbal praise on its own is not very effective in reinforcing canine behaviour. This is important for you, because

Games can be very motivating.

you need to know that you must provide your Labrador with something more valuable than 'Good dog' if you want him to learn to do as you say. Dogs need motivation – this is our third principle of training – and to motivate a dog, we need to ascertain what our dogs genuinely find rewarding.

In early training sessions, the simplest rewards are food, and often, the messiest foods are the most effective reinforcers – sardines, warm roast-meat dripping in juices. Obviously, it is easier to carry and store dry biscuits, but there will be times when you need to use messy food. Later on, as training progresses, you'll be able to use toys and opportunities to retrieve as rewards for your dog. Outside of training sessions, you will have lots of opportunities to reinforce desirable behaviours by making sure that your dog gets what he wants at the precise moment when he does something that you want him to do. This could be as simple as the dog looking at you (something you want) before you open the door and let him into the garden (something he wants). You could go a bit further and ask him to sit first. You can build lots of great behaviour and good manners with simple acts of opportunistic training throughout the day.

Positive-reinforcement training

The correct term for modern dog training is *positive*-reinforcement training, not just reinforcement. A lot of people think the word positive here stands for happy or fun. It doesn't – it is a mathematical term. There are actually two types of reinforcement used in animal training: not only can you reinforce behaviour by adding something that the dog likes, you can also reinforce behaviour by taking away something that the dog doesn't like. The former is called positive (something added) reinforcement, the latter is called negative (something taken away) reinforcement. Negative reinforcement is not something that we use much in dog training in the UK. Instead, we rely on positive reinforcement, or the use of rewards.

There are a couple of myths flying around about positive-reinforcement training, which we should probably put to bed. One is that positive training, as it is often called, is permissive training. In fact, being permissive with a dog is not training at all. Labradors are large dogs and need to be controlled, so a permissive approach is not appropriate. Just like traditionally trained dogs, all Labradors trained successfully with positive reinforcement have had months of effort and time put into them. No successful method of training is a quick fix.

The other myth I often come across is that positive training requires people to wave food about in order to get their dogs to obey them, and that if they don't have any food about their person, the dog will please himself. This is not the case. Effective dog training creates *responses* to *cues* (for example, a recall to a whistle) by reinforcing desirable behaviours. It does not use food as a signal to the dog that he needs to obey. Waving food at dogs to change their behaviour is usually a form of bribery, not training. With the exception of luring, which we'll discuss below, food is used as a reinforcer, never as a management tool.

Controlling rewards

You cannot teach a dog to come to your whistle if, on hearing it, he is able to ignore you and play with another dog instead. Play is highly reinforcing for many Labradors and they will repeat the behaviour that immediately preceded or accompanied the play. If that behaviour happens to be *ignoring your whistle*, you are in trouble. You *have* to be able to choose when your dog gets to play, or when he has any other reward, and the best way to do this outdoors is often with the judicious use of a training lead. This is not something you hold on to, but rather something that your dog trails behind him at all times so that he simply forgets he is wearing it. It is there simply for you to prevent him self-rewarding undesirable behaviours.

Controlling access to rewards is your fourth principle. Attaching your dog to a training lead only at times when you think he will disobey is not a good idea because it allows him to become wise to your game. So if you use one, you need to do so for an extended period of time, often for many months. This gives you and the dog a chance to relax and learn some great new behaviours in challenging environments – public parks, for example – without the risk of losing control.

When you start training, you will find that your dog learns quickly at home with nothing to disturb the pair of you, but that his ability to concentrate flies out of the window when he gets excited.

Dealing with excitement

Your next principle is to keep your Labrador 'under threshold'. I'll explain what that means. Labradors are very enthusiastic dogs. If they like something, they don't just like it, they *love* it with a passion. This can lead to dogs, especially young dogs, getting very excited and overwrought, especially if they can see the object of their desires but are being denied access to it. Think of the Labrador on a lead who wants to play with another dog. He leaps about, oblivious to the pain of the collar on his throat as he jerks at the end of the lead. There comes a point for any dog when he is so excited that he can no longer respond to his owner or the cues he is being given. Bawling, 'SIT!', 'DOWN!', 'NO!', or hurling expletives, will have little effect on the dog. This has nothing at all to do with obedience. *In that moment*, your dog is not aware of food or pain, so neither bribery nor mild punishment are likely to have any effect at all on his behaviour. Behaviourists refer to a dog in this state as being 'over threshold'. Let's have a closer look.

Behaviour thresholds

Behaviour thresholds are the point at which desirable behaviour begins to break down in the presence of a distraction. The more complicated the behaviour or response you want from your dog, the more likely he is to be unable to respond in the presence of a distraction. So, for example, your dog might be able to touch your hand on cue in the presence of another dog, but be unable to maintain the sit/stay for any length of time. Training raises behaviour thresholds to enable the dog to perform in the presence of distractions.

A dog that is over threshold cannot absorb information and is incapable of learning. He may be moving uncontrollably (lunging about at the end of a lead) or literally frozen into immobility, eyes fixed, muscles quivering. You can wave your hand in front of this dog's eyes and he won't see it. You can stick food under his nose and he probably won't even sniff it. I see people trying to train dogs in this state, and it is completely pointless.

We can only train a dog that is under threshold, and one way to help bring your dog back under threshold is to move him farther away from whatever is distracting him. Even when a dog does not seem to be particularly excited, he may be unable to respond to a cue that you give him if he is too close to a new or interesting distraction. Distractions are not the only factors that influence the difficulty of a task that you ask your dog to carry out. The distance between you and your dog, and the duration of the activity you are asking him to engage in, are important factors, too. We often refer to these as the three Ds of dog training.

The three Ds of dog training

Distance, distraction and duration are all factors that increase the challenge or complexity of a task. When increased individually, any of them may reduce the dog's ability to perform a known skill. When increased in *combination*, it is highly likely that your dog will fail. One of the most common mistakes made by dog owners is to try to raise the bar too quickly, often taking huge leaps from dog owners is to try to raise the bar too quickly, often taking huge leaps from the very simple to the most difficult tasks, which the dog is expected to perform. Each of the three Ds needs to be trained in incremental steps separately from the others, then re-combined. This is often referred to as proofing.

Proofing

Many people teach their puppy to sit for two seconds, and think they have taught him to sit. They haven't. They have simply taught him to sit *for two seconds*. Dogs don't generalise well, and assume if you teach two seconds, two seconds is what you want. If you leave them there for ten seconds, they'll get up and wander off. This is not disobedience. It's a breakdown in communication. Teaching a dog to hold a position such as sit for a longer period of time (duration), or to walk to heel past the neighbour's cat (distraction) or recall from the other side of your local playing field (distance) are all types of proofing. If you proof your dog training carefully, you'll be in an important minority of dog owners, and you will have a very well-trained dog. It takes a bit of effort, but it is well worth it.

One at a time

To proof your training, you need to increase one of the three Ds, and when you do this, you need to make the other two easier. If you teach your dog to sit for one minute at home with you alone (as you should) and then ask him to sit for one minute when your visitors arrive, you are setting him up to fail. Always make duration or distance shorter when you add a distraction, and vice versa. So, if you are adding the distraction of a visitor, you need to reduce the duration of the task to begin with. Ask for a three-second sit when the visitors arrive and then reward him. When the three Ds are increased one at a time, and in small increments, it is easy for the dog to succeed.

🐾 Dog-training equipment

You don't need much equipment to train a dog at a basic level. A harness with a long training lead attached to it will be needed for proofing. You'll need a treat bag to attach to your belt or around your waist. Once you get outdoors, you'll need a reward toy, such as a tennis ball. You'll need some signals, too – a whistle and a clicker are very useful.

People get in a bit of a muddle over clickers and whistles. 'Should I use a clicker train or whistle train?' they ask, which is actually a bit like saying, 'What do I need to write a letter – a pen or some paper?' Whistles and clickers have different roles. A whistle is a cue – it tells the dog, 'Do this.' A clicker is an event marker – it tells the dog, 'I liked it when you did that.'

We use event markers to identify for the dog exactly the behaviour he is being rewarded for. It can be difficult otherwise to reinforce the right behaviour. Imagine trying to reinforce a dog for holding something in his mouth if he holds it for one second only, or for touching something with his paw if the touch is fleeting. Yet it is from these tiny actions that we build up complex chains of behaviours, so we need to be able to tell the dog, 'Yes, you got it right.' You can actually do this with a word such as 'yes' or 'good', but a clicker is much more precise and consistent than the human voice.

Basic training requires very little equipment.

An event marker is given its power by pairing it with something that the dog finds reinforcing, such as food. You need to make sure that this association is well established before you begin training. We call this process 'charging' the clicker and it simply means making a click and throwing a treat to the dog, several times in succession, so that when he hears the sound, he expects a treat.

Practical skills

There are some practical skills you'll need to acquire in order to train your new friend. The three most important are luring, capturing and shaping.

Luring

Luring simply means getting a dog to follow a morsel of food with the end of his nose. This is useful behaviour because it enables us to move a dog into different positions and locations without pushing or pulling him around. We can lure a dog into a sit, for example, or on to a mat or over a jump.

In times gone by, this part of training was achieved by 'modelling', which meant manipulating the dog into the required position while giving him a command. Unfortunately, the dog's natural reaction to being pulled or pushed is to resist. This uses the very opposite group of muscles that we need him to use in order to get him into the position that we want. Luring speeds up the process of learning new positions by linking our cue with the correct muscle activity.

The key to successful use of the lure is to use it and lose it as quickly as possible. You don't want the lure to become the cue. So lure your dog two or three times and then show him that your lure hand is empty and mimic the luring movement as if you are still holding food. These fake lures can then easily be morphed into hand signals.

Capturing

Capturing involves observing the dog, seeing him do something you like and marking it with a clicker or word. For example, you could sit in your kitchen with a cup of coffee and watch your dog. If he lies down, you could mark that action with a click and throw a treat so that he has to get up again to reach it. In a while, if he lies down again, you can mark the down and reward him just as before. Sooner or later, he will catch on and start throwing himself into a down position for more treats. Capturing cannot be hurried and is best attempted when you have time on your hands.

Shaping

Shaping is an amazing process. This is how complex behaviours are established. We identify one action that the dog is capable of and that can be developed into something bigger and better. We lure or capture that action until the dog does it repeatedly. We then stop reinforcing the dog and wait for him to exaggerate the action, or change it slightly. For example, if we want him to pick up a toy, we might first reinforce him for looking at the toy. Just a glance will do.

When we stop reinforcing that look, he will become impatient, and if we wait, he will eventually, in exasperation, exaggerate the action. This might involve a step towards the toy, or even poking it with his nose, as if to say, 'See! I'm looking.' Now is our chance. We capture this new behaviour and give him his treat. The bar has been raised and he now has to go towards the toy or poke it to earn a reward. Shaping can elegantly build brand-new behaviours and I'll be helping you to practise this useful skill in the next chapter.

🐾 Teach him to DO, not to STOP doing

When you start training your dog, you'll have two main objectives. You'll want to stop him doing things you don't want him to do, and you'll want to teach him to do things you do want him to do, on your signal or command. Every home is different. For example, you might want to stop your dog jumping on the sofa while another family might not care. There's no right and wrong here. Bear in mind, though, that if you want him to be a welcome house guest, it's probably a good idea not to allow behaviours that most people won't like.

Traditional dog training placed heavy emphasis on stopping bad behaviours. *Don't* get on the sofa, *don't* put your paws on the counter, *don't* jump up at Uncle Jim in his new suit. Stopping a dog doing something he enjoys can be done in two ways. Either we can apply an aversive – making the consequence of his behaviour unpleasant – or we can ask him for an alternative and more desirable behaviour. Applying aversives is the use of punishment, and we've already touched on some of the disadvantages of using punishment in dog training. Another problem with this approach is that there are so many different options for the dog. Okay, he can't put his paws on the counter, so he'll put them on the table; he can't steal your shoe, so he'll steal your cushion, instead. It isn't uncommon to see a dog work through a whole range of different ways to be bad in the space of a few minutes, while his unwitting owner's temper becomes increasingly frayed. This is how nice Labradors earn nasty labels: naughty, dominant, willful, spoilt. The answer is to focus on a suitable alternative behaviour, and on management strategies to help us cope when we are not training.

So we don't try to stop the dog begging at the table; we teach him to sit on his mat while we are eating. We don't try to stop the dog lying on the sofa; we put a basket next to it and teach him to relax in there. In the meantime, we put a baby gate across the sitting-room door so that he can't get up to mischief when we don't feel like training.

Focus on DO rather than DON'T. Do is not a cop out, and it isn't spoiling your dog. Managing your dog when you are not training him is common sense. Remember, your dog is always learning. He stores the consequences of each of his actions in his brain and it calculates which are his most beneficial activities so that he can pursue them more thoroughly in the future. If you are not in control of his consequences, the consequences for you may be surprising. Bad habits build fast.

Dogs can't get into the habit of chewing stuff they can't reach, and teaching dogs good context-based behaviours (sit to be petted, lie down while we eat) reduces conflict in the home and helps to make your dog welcome when he steps outside it.

Learn and practise

Let's recap. Here are the seven principles to guide you as you train your Labrador:

- **If you are a dog owner, you are a dog trainer.**
- **Dogs do what benefits them.**
- **You need to motivate your dog in order to train him.**
- **Always control your dog's access to rewards.**
- **Keep your dog under threshold when training.**
- **Add the three Ds in incremental steps.**
- **Teach your dog to DO, not to STOP doing.**

Many people wonder how super-successful dog trainers get such amazing results. The truth is, all successful dog trainers follow these principles, and they practise a great deal. A big part of dog-training success is simply turning up, putting in the hours. Spend some time really understanding the principles of how dogs learn as well as teaching him. Read as much about dog training as you can. You'll find some great resources in the back of this book. Join my online forum for support and help from other Labrador owners from all over the world. Then practise and practise your basic training techniques. Become proficient with a clicker and a lure. It doesn't take long, and if you start off practising with a few simple tricks, you'll be thoroughly competent by the time you come to training the important stuff. Just remember, to the dog, it's all a game. He'll be happy just to play along.

We've had a look at the how and why of dog training, so let's move on now and have a look at the what and the when. In the next chapter, we are going to talk about what to teach, and in what order. We'll put principles into practice and get you started with training your dog.

10

Practical training: the basics

Labradors are big strong dogs, and, despite the Labrador's winning nature, having 36kg (80lb) of undisciplined dog drag you around, or completely ignore you, is an ultimately depressing experience and one that will close a lot of doors to both of you. Your dog needs training, and the very best time to make a start is today.

In the previous chapter, we looked at the theory and principles of dog training. In this chapter, we are going to jump in and learn some practical skills. You'll probably want to teach your dog to sit, come when he is called and walk next to you without pulling on his lead. These are very basic obedience requirements for any dog, and essential if you are to have control over your Labrador. We are not, however, going to begin our training programme with these three commands. We'll be starting with some simple exercises first, to build your skills as much as your dog's, and to set you on the path to success. I'll explain what the purpose of each one is as we go.

Food manners

As we are going to be training with edible rewards initially, one of the first things to take care of is the way your dog behaves around food. It is very difficult to make any progress with training if your dog is putting all his efforts into launching an all-out assault on your treat bag or pot. So the first exercise we tackle is 'Don't grab'. This is all about teaching the dog not to snatch food from your bag, container or hands. It also teaches you to observe your dog closely, react swiftly and wait patiently for changes in behaviour. Start each exercise standing up, and finish by sitting on the floor.

From the hand

Put half a dozen tiny pieces of food in the palm of your hand and close your fist over them. Hold the closed fist out to your dog and wait for him to stop licking and pawing at it. As soon as he backs off a little, start to uncurl your fingers. Curl them up again as he moves towards your hand, uncurl them as he moves away. He'll soon back off so that you can open your

Learning to be patient around food is a key skill.

hand fully. With your other hand, take one treat from the open palm and give it to the dog. You may have to stop and start this a few times so that he learns to wait while you take the treat and place it against his lips.

Repeat this process kneeling down, and then sitting on the floor. Keep practising until the dog makes no attempt to get food from your hand in any of these positions.

From a container

This time, have your treats in a small pot with a narrow top that you can cover with your hand. To begin with, each time you uncover the pot, the dog may attempt to get at the contents. Simply place your hand over the pot again and wait for him to back off.

Start standing up with the pot held at your waist. When the dog backs off, take a treat from the pot and give it to him. Any attempt to snatch, and the treat goes back in the pot again. Progress to sitting on a chair with the pot on your lap, then to the floor. When your dog is able to watch you uncover the pot on your lap while you are sitting on the floor, and to wait patiently while you take a treat from the pot and press it to his lips, you can start to place the pot on the floor. Be ready to cover the pot with your hand if the dog tries to get at the treat.

You'll soon be able to place the pot anywhere – on the floor or on a low surface – and the dog will ignore it and wait for you to offer him a piece of the food. If your dog needs a lot of practice, you can use most of his meals to get this right. Behaving appropriately around food is an essential component of your dog's education and well worth mastering before moving on to any other training.

❀ The hand touch

In this simple exercise, we are going to teach the dog to target your hand. He is literally going to bump the palm of your hand with the tip of his nose whenever you ask him to. The hand target is a simple and useful exercise to complete. It teaches you how to use a clicker, and gives you an opportunity to build your skill in using this event marker. You'll learn to observe your dog closely and concentrate on his body movements, and to click in a timely manner. It can seem as though you need an extra hand initially, but with practice, you will soon be using this important tool efficiently.

Hand targeting teaches the dog that he can control the flow of rewards from you to him, and it can be used to open lines of communication between you and the dog in distracting situations. In the previous chapter, we talked about behaviour thresholds, and how in some situations your dog will be too distracted and/ or excited to respond to your cues. You've all seen the friendly young dog bouncing around visitors while his owner tries in vain to get him to Sit, *sit*, SIT! He is too excited to respond. He is, in fact, over threshold. In situations like this, we sometimes need to lower our requirements. To ask the dog to do something less demanding, briefer, not so much of a big deal, is more likely to get a response. The hand touch brings the dog back to focusing on working with you to earn rewards.

Hand targeting is also a useful component of two other important skills: the recall and the retrieve.

What does the exercise involve?

You are going to use your hand as a cue or signal that you want the dog to bump the centre of your palm with his nose. When you use a part of your body as a signal, it must be clear and unambiguous. So, in this case, your hand will be held out flat, fingers together, palm facing the dog, fingers pointing towards the floor. Each cue consists of a brief presentation of the hand in this position, lasting three seconds. You withdraw your hand at the end of three seconds and rest it on your lap, or put it behind your back, if you wish. There should be a clear difference between the hand as a signal and the hand in-between signals. You mark the exact moment the dog does what you want him to do, and follow that mark with an edible reward.

Preparation

You'll need an event marker for this exercise (see Chapter 9, Principles of Labrador training). A clicker is ideal. You'll also need some treats in a pot on a low table, or in your treat bag. Make sure there are no distractions around you.

Work in a quiet room, just you and the dog. If your dog shows no interest in touching your hand when you first present it to him, rub a tiny piece of cheese or peanut butter onto a small area, the size of a 20p piece, in the centre of your palm. It may help if you practise presenting the palm of your hand clearly in front of a mirror before involving your dog. Make a loose fist, then smartly open your hand nice and flat, fingers together, then make a loose fist again. Practise switching neatly between fist and palm to make a clear, unambiguous signal.

Training

Present your hand to your dog – hold it a few centimetres (a couple of inches) from his nose and wait for him to move his nose towards your palm. Use your clicker or marker word to mark the exact moment when the dog moves his nose towards your palm. Don't wait for him to touch it. Immediately reward the dog with a tiny piece of food. Repeat several times. Then, on the next presentation of your hand, wait for actual contact with his nose. Mark and reward as before. After several more repetitions, you can start to ask the dog to make a bit more effort.

Begin to present your hand a bit farther away from the dog, so that he has to take a step or two forwards before bumping your palm with his nose. If he doesn't touch when you increase the distance, simply remove your hand. There is no reward this time. Next time, make it easier by holding your hand a bit closer.

Changing positions

When your dog presses his nose to your hand each time you present it, the next step is to try holding your hand in different positions. Sometimes to the right of the dog, sometimes to his left, sometimes above, so he has to lift and move his head around in order to make contact with your palm. This helps him to understand that the target is the palm of your hand, wherever that may happen to be, not just in a few limited positions. Understanding that a target is still a target, even when it is in a different place, is an important step.

Changing locations

Finally, you can try the exercise in different locations, and even introduce a few distractions. Start with different rooms in the house, then try it in the garden. If your dog struggles in new locations, make the exercise easier again. Now add some distractions. Start him off with a few simple distractions around the house. Ask for a hand touch when there is someone else in the room, then when someone familiar is stroking him. Work up to more challenging distractions gradually, and start varying the rewards. Instead of always rewarding with food, start using opportunities around you. Ask him for a hand touch before you open the door for him to go into the garden, before you give him his dinner and before you throw his ball.

Teaching the recall

Recall is one of the most important skills you will ever teach your dog. It is very easy to teach a dog to come when you call him at home. Proofing that recall against distractions outdoors is another matter. This can be a long process. The secret lies in building up gradually, setting your dog up to win and controlling the consequences of ignoring you. If a dog ignores a recall command, you need to do two things:

- **Ensure he cannot get any kind of reward.**
- **Ensure you set up plenty of successful recalls for the next few days.**

Failure must be unrewarding for the dog and very infrequent. If you can stick to these two rules, you will have an excellent recall. The best way to ensure your dog cannot access rewards after ignoring a recall outdoors is to have him on a training line. Use high-value treats to get the recall going at each step. You can switch to lower-value treats once you are making progress, and remove the line when the dog's response is effortlessly fluent.

Stage one – engineer your recalls

Forget about whistles and don't call your dog. The first step of the recall is to engineer lots of situations where your dog runs after you. A good way to get a dog coming towards you is to attract his attention with a squeaky noise, then back or walk away from him. Most dogs will chase after you if you act a bit silly and then run around your garden. As soon as you have engineered this recall behaviour, turn and face the dog. When he is almost at your side, present your hand in the target position. Click and treat him for touching it. If he fails to touch your hand, go back to your hand-targeting lessons for a day or two and then try again.

Stage two – associate a cue

Once you have got your dog enjoying running after you, it is time to associate a cue with this action. Do not be tempted to use this cue to trigger the recall. That is stage three. First, we are going to build a nice strong association between your cue and the act of running full pelt towards you. Spend several days on this in your house and garden. Get your dog chasing you. Then and only then, just before he reaches you, give your cue – come, or pip pip pip pip on the whistle.

Training should be fun.

Stage three – responding to the cue

Here's the part where you get your dog to respond to your cue. He needs to have had lots of practice (weeks) at the previous step before you introduce this one. Wait for a time when he is not distracted, and deliver your cue. Get that hand touch as he arrives, say 'Yes' and feed him something really nice. Repeat in different parts of the house and garden every day.

Stage four is the part where we proof your recall command, and the rest of your obedience training, so that your dog will recall absolutely anywhere and under any circumstances. We'll look at proofing your new skills in a moment, but, first, let's look at establishing that other very important command, the sit, and also walking to heel.

Establishing the sit

Sit is a great command because it is an excellent default behaviour for any dog. We talked in the previous chapter about the importance of focusing on behaviours we want rather than on behaviours we don't want. Sit is a good replacement for undesirable behaviours, such as jumping up, and it is one of the easiest skills to teach. Luring and capturing are both great ways to get a dog into the sitting position. We'll start with luring because you'll need to use this should your dog ignore your cue later on. Just like recall, we establish the position first. Don't say 'Sit' while you do this.

Stage one (a) – luring the sit

In this exercise, we'll be using a lure to get the dog into the sitting position and a clicker to mark, reward and release him. As always when we lure a dog, we need to remember our 'use it and lose it' rule. Don't keep luring – use the lure three or four times, then mimic the luring action with an empty hand.

Hold the food lure in one hand, bring it close to the dog's nose and lift it slowly over his head and backwards in the direction of his tail. As the dog lifts his nose to follow the lure, his bottom will automatically come down into a sit. All you have to do is mark the sit with your clicker (or a verbal 'Yes') and give him the treat. Now let's try capturing.

Stage one (b) – capturing the sit

If you have a dog in front of you, and some treats in your hand, the chances are the dog will sit. All you need to do is click with your clicker, and throw the treat away from the dog so that he has to get up again in order to get it. This then gives him an opportunity to offer another sit, and earn another reward. A few happy sessions like this with ten or twenty treats and you can move on to step two.

Stage two – associating the cue

Now it's time to say 'Sit' as your dog drops into the sit position. Remember, you are naming the sit, not asking for one. As he starts to sit, you give it a name. Think of it as a language lesson rather than a test of obedience. After a few days of naming that sit, you can go to step three and teach him to respond to the cue.

Stage three – responding to the cue

Now you can start *asking* for a sit. Pick your occasions carefully. Ask your dog to sit often, but make it easy for him to succeed, with nothing to distract him. If he does not sit immediately after you give the sit cue, simply lure him into a sit and reward him as normal. Then make sure you set up the next exercise to be even easier. Don't add distractions until you have a very reliable response to your cue without them.

Walk next to me

Walking to heel is one of those skills that some owners find more difficult than any other, but it needn't be that way. The secret to success is to forget all about going for a walk with the dog next to you, but to focus instead on a) getting him into the right position and b) holding that position for just a very few steps.

There are several ways to get a dog into the heel position. Let's look at two of them.

Stage one – shaping the heel position

You can shape the position by imagining a big circle (around about two metres/ six feet across) on the ground. The circle is attached to your left foot so that everywhere you go, the circle goes too. Now walk around in an enclosed area, such as a large room, or on a paved area in your garden, such as a patio or drive. Click and treat the dog each time he enters your circle, and keep walking around. Throw the treat outside the circle so that the dog has to leave the circle to collect it, and come back into the circle to earn his next reward. Make the circle smaller as the dog improves, and don't walk far once the dog is in position. Two or three steps, then click and treat.

Stage two (a) – adding a cue

There are several ways to cue heel. Once your circle is small, you can start using the word 'heel' each time the dog moves into it. He will soon come to associate this word with walking closely at your side. You can also use a hand signal, such as a pat of your hip. The most important cue for heel is the presence of a lead.

Stage two (b) – adding a lead

The lead makes this exercise more formal, but don't be tempted to go charging off on long lead walks with your dog just yet. Remember, the key to good heel- work is getting those first two or three steps right. Once you clip on a lead, you can no longer reward him by throwing the treat outside your circle. So now, we will simply reinforce the dog in the heel position as we walk along.

If the dog seems unsure about the heel position with the lead on, or moves out of the correct position, stop moving. Pat your hip, lure the dog back into position with a treat and try again. Remember to lose the lure after two or three repeti- tions and stop and treat the dog after two or three steps.

Stage three – responding to the cue

Every time you attach a lead to your dog, he should maintain the heel position for as long as the lead is attached. Of course, two or three steps at heel is not going to get you to the park and back. In fact, it isn't going to get you very far at all. Let's look at the practical steps involved in adding duration and distractions to this and other new behaviours.

Proofing obedience

In the previous chapter, we talked about the three Ds: distance, duration and distraction. In the real world, life is not quite so simple as saying 'Sit' or 'Come' to a dog and rewarding him when he arrives. Events and circumstances conspire to interfere with your training, and your dog should be able to sustain a sit or heel position for more than a few seconds, both with and without the presence of distractions. We'll take a look at adding some duration first. For this, we are going to use a technique I call treat streaming.

Duration and treat streaming

One of the key mistakes most people make when training with food is to reward too infrequently at first. This is especially true when we begin building duration into behaviours, and it's very important that you take care with this when building duration into your sit and heel positions. Treat streaming means literally feeding treats one after another in a stream, at one-second intervals to begin with.

Obviously, it's important that you don't make your dog fat. This is unlikely since you'll be treat streaming for a short time only, but nevertheless it's best to deduct food used in training from your dog's daily allowance.

The short stay

'Sit', is a pretty pointless command if the dog just gets straight up again. In fact, almost every sit has some kind of duration to it. The stay is simply a longer duration sit or down. You don't need a separate stay command for this and I recommend you don't use one. It's easy to teach a sit/stay if you are generous with your treats. From now on, the rule is that Sit means, 'Sit and don't move until I say so.' The dog does not get up until he hears your release cue. You can say, 'Go play', 'Free', 'Okay', or anything else you feel is appropriate.

Ask your dog to sit, and instead of the click and treat, feed him as he sits. Then release him with your cue. Throw the treat away from him, so he has to move about a bit, then ask him to sit again. This time give him three treats, one after the other at one-second intervals, then release him.

Now repeat, increasing the number of treats to ten (and, therefore, the length of the stay to ten seconds). Now you can begin to increase the gaps between your treats to two seconds. Go back to a shorter sit to begin with, four seconds is fine. Release with your cue, treat and then ask him to sit again. Finish each session with a shorter stay and more frequent treats. Ending on an easy and successful note is always important when building duration.

Adding duration to your heelwork

The principles here are exactly the same. Set off with your dog at heel, stop and feed every two or three steps. Now see if you can manage to feed him on the move. Do six steps, feeding every two steps from your left hand. Deliver the food with your hand behind your hip. Build up to ten steps, feeding every two turns, walk in a square, walk in a circle. Practise on your patio or driveway, practise on your lawn. Keep practising.

When your dog is really fluent, you can start to reduce the frequency of your rewards. Give one every four or five steps, then one every six or seven steps and so on, until you can walk ten steps perfectly without a break and with no reinforcements.

Now it is time to add some distractions, and when we do, we will be going right back to treat streaming all over again. Adding distractions takes a little planning and a little help from your friends.

Distraction – fake it till you make it

Letting things just happen with an untrained or part-trained dog is a recipe for disaster. Don't wait until your dog happens to be playing with other dogs in the park to practise his recall. The chances of failure are almost 100 per cent. Every new level of difficulty you challenge your dog to face should be practised in controlled conditions first. This gives you the best chance of success.

The point of the fake conditions is to ensure you can control the outcome of your experiment. Setting up fake training scenarios at home and in public places in this way is a vital part of successful dog training, but you cannot do it all alone. If your dog behaves badly around other dogs, you will need a friend with a dog, so that you can practise how to behave near other dogs. If your dog loves kids, you will need to borrow some children from whom to call him away (with their parents' permission, of course). During much of this faking process, you will need a rock-solid means of preventing your dog helping himself to rewards should he ignore your cues. This means putting your dog in a harness and attaching a training lead to it until he is absolutely reliable in his responses. It is vital that your dog is not able to help himself to rewards.

The kinds of rewards that Labradors will commonly attempt to take for themselves after behaving inappropriately are games with other dogs, running up to strangers and jumping up at them, joining in children's games uninvited, chasing leaves and so on. Anything that your dog enjoys doing can be used by him *as a reward*. It is important to recognise that when rewards follow naughtiness, that naughtiness is reinforced. In other words, it is more likely to happen again. The training lead is your friend during the proofing process, because it helps you prevent the dog grabbing these rewards after being naughty. It puts you where you should be – in charge of all the good things that happen to your dog.

Let's look at a common problem as an example – the dog that will not walk nicely on a lead past other dogs. Remember, we talked about increasing the power of distractions incrementally. Other dogs running free are the greatest challenge.

So we start our training with a distraction dog sitting still on his lead. If you have a friend who is training her dog, too, you can take turns to be the distraction dog.

Seated-distraction dog

Ask your friend to sit her dog next to her, six to 10 metres (20 to 30 feet) away from you. This is the seated-distraction dog. Now you need to behave as though the other dog is not there. Practise lead-walking up and down, well away from your friend and her dog. Do not approach them. Have some tasty treats in a bag attached to your belt and reinforce the dog frequently for holding the heel position.

Walk in a neat circle or square, walk up and down an imaginary line, stop and start, ask your dog to sit every now and then. Keep him focused and concentrating on you. When he is successful, and only then, you can move three metres (10 feet) nearer to your friend and repeat. Gradually, work your way nearer until your dog can heel in a square around and close to your friend. This may take several sessions, depending on your dog.

Once your dog has mastered this, practise for a while with fewer and/or lower-value treats. Now you can make things a little harder by setting the distraction dog into motion. Remember the three Ds: duration, distraction, distance – every time we increase one D, we make the others easier. So put some more distance between you and the distraction by moving right back to 10 metres (30 feet) away.

Moving-distraction dog

This time, have your friend walk her own dog up and down in a small area 10 metres (30 feet) away, while you do the same with your dog. Each dog must focus on his own handler, and not on the other dog. Use high-value treats and sufficient distance to ensure success. Gradually, as the dogs succeed, bring them closer together, until, eventually, you can have one dog making a small circle inside the circle made by the other dog. Have the two dogs moving in opposite directions so they have to walk past facing each other.

Vary the drills and keep practising. Try walking up and down an imaginary line with you and your dog on one side, and your friend and her dog on the other. Reduce the space between the dogs, until they almost brush past one another without breaking focus on their handlers. Getting to this point takes time. Depending on the dogs, it will take several sessions.

All training, including your sit/stay and your recall, needs to be proofed in this way. A very detailed explanation of the proofing process with lots of examples of fake training scenarios may be found in my book *Total Recall*, which focuses on teaching this learning and proofing process through that single skill. These kinds of exercises can also be practised in a good outdoor-training class. Check the Association of Pet Dog Trainers website for training sessions in your area.

So far, we have looked at duration and distraction. Now let's briefly look at that third D – distance.

Building distance

The term distance refers to the distance between the handler and the dog. As always, when we make one D more difficult, the others must be made simpler. Obedience at a distance, such as recalling the dog from 100 metres (100 yards) away, must be taught away from distractions. Only when he is rock solid in two different aspects should you attempt to combine them.

We can add distance to the sit in two ways. We can ask the dog to sit when he is at a distance, or we can leave him on the sit/stay and walk some distance away from him. The former is an advanced skill and we'll look at that in Chapter 13, Advanced training, activities and sports. Walking away from the dog on a sit/ stay should not be attempted until you have added plenty of duration to the sit at your side. The fact that you are moving at all is a challenge for many dogs, so proof your dog against your movement by starting with small body movements and work up to bigger ones. Take little steps back and forth and to the side and all around the dog before you start to move away from him. At first, return frequently to release and treat him.

Any problems?

If you have worked your way through these skill stages with a young puppy, you probably won't have many of the issues addressed in the next chapter. But it may be that you have an older puppy or young dog that has already got into some bad habits. Most of the issues you are likely to be experiencing can be resolved with a little time and patience. Don't blame yourself for any mistakes you may have made. Training a dog is a complex and quite challenging process. Try to look ahead and put aside a little time each day for retraining your dog. If you have read this far, you'll have some idea where you went wrong, and the next chapter will give you the guidelines you need for putting things right.

11

Growing up and adolescence

As your Labrador passes the six-month mark, many of the problems of puppyhood begin to disappear. No longer are your fingers used as a teething ring. No puddles should be appearing on the floor, and no more trips to the garden in the wee small hours. In their place, however, can emerge a new raft of challenges to keep you on your toes.

It is very common for new dog owners to find that their training begins to fall apart when their puppy gets to eight or nine months old. He starts ignoring his owner, running off, playing with other dogs, jumping all over people and disobeying commands that he knows perfectly well. If your dog is behaving badly in one of these ways, you may be wondering if he is trying to become the dominant member of your partnership. We're going to take a look at this concern and at some of the common problems people experience with young dogs approaching maturity.

A word about dominance

For a long time, it was widely believed that dogs were pack animals and, in a group situation, would organise themselves into a hierarchy with an alpha dog at the top. Trainers attempted to replicate the behaviour of the alpha dog in order to pre-empt any attempts by their domestic dog to overthrow his human master as leader of the pack.

The theory behind this belief was based on our observations and studies of groups of (unrelated) captive wolves, and the way in which they behaved towards one another. More recently, several studies have turned this theory on its head. We now know much more about the behaviour of wolves that are living naturally in the wild. We know, for example, that wolf packs are actually families of closely related animals, usually led by a parent. There is little jostling for position, and a great deal of co-operation and teamwork.

We also know that feral dogs living on the fringes of civilisation do not form packs or hierarchies at all. Outbreaks of fighting among dogs are almost always related to a shortage of resources. The truth is that dogs, and even wolves, are, for the most part, not even slightly interested in dominance. They are interested in survival and in their home comforts. Dogs and wolves don't alpha roll one another, and you won't need to alpha roll your dog in order to be in charge.

Boisterous and rough behaviour

One of the most common complaints I hear from owners of young Labradors going through the hooligan stage, is that their dog is becoming increasingly rough, sometimes to the point where the owner is becoming afraid of the dog. The kinds of behaviour involved may vary from leaping excitedly into the air around the owner, air snapping with clicking teeth near faces, or even nipping and tearing at the owner's clothing.

Labradors are powerful dogs.

Although he looks quite grown up, an eight-month-old dog is still very much a puppy, and puppies like to play rough. The first course of action to take with a boisterous dog of this kind is to stop *all* hands-on physical play between the dog and people. If you start a physical game, the dog *will* get excited, and he *will* attempt to escalate the game when you attempt to end it. Focus instead on interacting with the dog through training and structured games, such as fetch, where you are in control of the toy, and where you choose when the game starts and stops.

Have your dog on a harness and training line when he is outdoors, so that you have control over him, and stop all interaction with the dog if he starts getting rough. At the same time, you need to establish a good training relationship with your dog. A training relationship is one where the dog understands you are the ultimate source of rewards, and he can earn those rewards by pleasing you. It is actually surprisingly easy to establish this relationship with any dog through clicker training, and this kind of attention-seeking behaviour will improve dramatically when you do so.

Some of the hardest problems to resolve arise with dogs that have little interest in their owner's attention. Instead, the dog focuses all his interest on other dogs.

Running after other dogs

In Chapter 10, Practical training: the basics, we looked at coping with distractions. For a Labrador, other dogs are one of the strongest distractions you could possibly dream up. The reason your recall breaks down when other dogs are around, is simply that recall training must include a proofing stage in which you teach your dog to recall away from things he finds attractive.

Don't panic if your dog goes deaf whenever he finds a friend to play with. This is very common and can be fixed. It involves taking a step back and teaching your dog to recall away from other dogs under very controlled conditions. If you have been using your recall whistle or verbal cue ('Come') a great deal while your dog has been off playing with other dogs, the behaviour pattern of ignoring your recall signals may have become highly reinforced, and you might want to consider retraining the recall from scratch, using a different signal.

Whether or not you start with a new signal, you'll need to set up lots of 'fake it till you make it' scenarios. Make the practice recalls easy for your dog to begin with and then gradually increase the level of difficulty, so that he is always able to win his reward. You will need to control the rewards (opportunities to play)

A good recall makes walking safe and fun.

by having him on a long line, so that access to them can be withdrawn or offered, depending on whether he responds to your cues.

People sometimes say to me, 'I haven't time for all that,' or, 'I don't know anyone who can help me,' and I'm afraid the answer is this: if you want your dog-friendly dog to recall away from other dogs, the only way to achieve this is by setting up situations for him to practise recalling away from other dogs, and for *you* totally to control the outcome. If you can't get friends to help you, you'll need to join a well-run dog-training class that offers outdoor recall sessions.

Pulling on the lead

The next common sticking point for owners of medium to large dogs, such as Labradors, is getting the dog to walk nicely on a loose lead. It is by no means unusual to see a hapless Labrador owner hurrying along in the dog's wake, clinging with outstretched arm to a taut lead at the end of which is a dog intent on choking himself – absolute misery for the owner, and potentially danger-ous. The reason that Labradors, and so many other dogs, pull hard on a lead is simple. It's because we reward them for doing so. 'Surely not!' you cry. 'I never reward my dog for pulling,' but actually, you do.

In the previous chapter, we talked about how rewards could be anything that the dog finds enjoyable or that he desires. Well, exercise is one of the biggest rewards you can offer your Labrador. Off-lead exercise is the icing on the cake, and what many people do is allow their dog to drag them, almost literally, all the way to the park or common, where they then proceed to give the dog the massive reward of being let off the lead. Think back to the last time you let your dog off the lead. Think about what he was doing before you undid that clip. As likely as not, what he was doing was *dragging* you towards his fun place. He knows he is about to get the best reward of the day, and, like many dogs, he is willing to endure some pain (hence the choking and gasping) in order to get rewards that he values highly, and which you provide for him in exchange for pulling.

You have two challenges ahead of you if you want your dog to stop pulling on the lead. The first is to stop reinforcing the pulling. Your job now is to *turn off those rewards* that you have been giving your dog for pulling and that means not indulging the dog *ever* after he has pulled on a lead. No dog should be given the pleasure of moving forwards, towards something he wants, if his lead is not slack. And he certainly should not have the pleasure of running free if the last thing he did was drag your arm from its socket.

Your second job is to start creating situations in which your dog can success-fully walk on a loose lead, and reinforce him for doing so. In an ideal world, from the moment you begin loose-lead training, your dog should never again be on a lead unless you are committed to remaining stationary each time he leaves your side. But what if you need to walk your dog to the vet? Or let him empty his blad-der in a lay-by during a long car journey? He will need to wear a lead then, for safety's sake.

This is where you may need a management solution – a way of reducing pull-ing and recovering control over your dog (and your dignity) when training is not possible, or not appropriate. A double-attachment body harness may be enough to stop some dogs pulling, others may need a head-collar. Bear in mind that some dogs find head-collars quite distressing to wear and will paw at them and try to get them off. A management solution is not a substitute for training. It should only ever be temporary and not a way of controlling your dog on a daily basis.

The secret to walking your dog on a loose lead successfully without the aid of harnesses or head-collars is this:

- **Stop rewarding your dog for pulling.**
- **Get the first two steps right.**

Once you have two steps on a loose lead, you can turn it into three. Once you have three, you can build them into five. But you have to get those first two steps right to start with. It's fine to use lots of treats to do this. You won't be dependent on them for the rest of eternity. Look again at the instructions in the previous chapter and remember to increase the reinforcement you give your dog for correct behaviours, and reduce the duration of your heelwork every time you make the task more difficult. In other words, *go back to treat streaming and two steps* with every single distraction you introduce.

Remember, going through gateways is a distraction, vehicles passing is a distraction, leaves blowing along the gutter, a place where another dog peed, these are all distractions. It might take you several days just to get to the end of your drive, or through your front gate to the pavement but, as you progress, it will get easier and easier. Ask friends to help you teach your dog to walk to heel past other dogs, his favourite toys, food, anything you can think of that might distract him. Take your time, step-by-step, and keep those treats flowing until the dog 'gets it'. It's worth the effort. Remember, it's okay to consider restricting your dog while you get this right. He won't come to any harm if he is mainly exercised in your garden for a week or two. Plenty of dogs survive for weeks on crate rest after injuries. It isn't ideal, but it might be the right solution for you.

Destructive behaviour and grim habits

We all expect small puppies to chew things up. That seems fair enough – they're teething, after all. But when you come home to find your ten-month-old has been ripping the plaster off your kitchen walls, you may wonder if your dog has something wrong with him. A significant cause of problems of this kind in young Labradors is that they have been de-crated too soon.

The truth is, Labradors are very mouthy dogs and youngsters often enjoy chewing anything and everything they can fit between their teeth. This can last

We need to channel all that energy.

for the best part of the first two years of their lives. The best way to avoid it is to crate the dog with a nice supply of frozen kongs to keep him happy while you are out. This stage doesn't last forever, and at some point, you will be able to ditch the crate. If you are leaving the dog too long for him to be crated, it may well be that his destructive behaviour is associated with too much time spent alone. A visit from a dog walker while you are out may provide the break and company that he needs.

Learning to be gentle is an important skill.

Not only do young Labradors enjoy chewing up inappropriate items, they also enjoy eating them. A common complaint from many new Labrador owners is that their dog eats his own faeces, or the faeces of other dogs, or the contents of discarded nappies, or other unmentionable products that some humans see fit to abandon in the countryside. At home, you have a good chance of success in stopping poop eating. You can ensure that poop is never left lying around and you can train your dog to come away from his freshly produced parcel by giving him a big reward each time he does so.

Out on walks, this behaviour can be a bit more challenging to resolve, since it is not always possible to know when the dog has found something unsuitable to swallow in time to intervene. If you can't change your walking area, you may need to use a muzzle to prevent him eating revolting substances. Try to take comfort from the fact that dogs are extremely resistant to pathogens that would make you and I very ill, and usually don't come to any harm from this horrible habit.

Your magic word

A magic word is one of my secret weapons. It can be yours, too. I think every Labrador between six and nine months of age should have a 'magic word'. It can be a real boost when dealing with a dog that picks up, touches and even eats inappropriate things. A magic word is an attention getter, an interrupter and an emergency recall all rolled into one. What it is, is a word so exciting to the dog that, whenever he hears it, he will stop whatever he is doing and come dashing to find you.

To generate your magic word, you will need some amazing treats. Tasty chunks of warm roast chicken dripping in juices, or whole sardines canned in oil are great examples – the messier and tastier the better. Once or twice each day, for several days, you will say your magic word and give your dog one of these fantastic prizes.

You won't ask the dog to do anything in return. The food is totally unconditional. All you want is for him to associate this word with an astounding experience. The first few times you give your dog the treat, go and find him, say your word and feed him straightaway. You don't want any delay at all in getting the food into his mouth immediately after he hears the word.

When he has heard the magic word a few times, you can start to say the word when he is a little way away from you. After the first few days, and once your dog has understood the deliciousness of this brilliant word, you can use your word less often. Twice a week should keep it special and ensure he does not forget it.

Choosing a word

Your word should be upbeat, cheerful and inspiring – 'hooray', 'awesome', 'eureka', that type of thing. It should sound celebratory. It means 'something wonderful and utterly unmissable is about to happen'.

Be careful. This is not a command. Don't use it to spoil his fun. Don't use your magic word to recall your dog from the garden, to stop him weeing on your geraniums, or to prevent him climbing on your sofa on a regular basis. It is your secret weapon, not an everyday tool. Each time you use the word to bring your dog away from something he wanted for himself, you deplete a little of its power. You make it just that little bit less magical. So do not use your word on a regular basis, or repeatedly, to try to trigger particular behaviours.

Emergencies only

Save your magic word for that awful time when your dog slips his lead and is about to run into the road. Save it for that walk on the beach when he finds a dead seagull and is about to eat it. Save it for the day he rolls in fox poo and is about to embrace your mother-in-law, or climb on her white sofa.

Save it for special and unusual occasions. Call out your magic word and feel the relief as your dog spins around and dashes towards you.

Recharging your magic word

When you have used your word, you need to recharge it to make it really special again. Don't use the word to interrupt your dog in something he enjoys for some time. And for the next few days, make sure you just say the word several times, together with an amazing treat, no strings attached.

Selective deafness

Adolescence is a time when many inexperienced Labrador owners really start to struggle generally with control issues, especially outdoors. The sweet little dog that was happy to trot about under their feet just a few short weeks earlier, and came running back whenever his name was called, has been replaced by a hooligan that divides his time between mugging strangers for their picnics and chasing squirrels. Commands that are meekly obeyed at home in the garden are treated with total contempt out in the wide world.

People often refer to their dogs as being 'selectively deaf'. In other words, he is choosing whether or not to obey. You are probably waiting for me to bring up that proofing word again here, because, of course, selective deafness is actually a lack of proofing. It can be tough to be constantly reminded that so many behaviours that we previously attributed to failings on the part of our dogs are, in actual fact, failings of the training process. In other words, they are the owner's fault. It's helpful for us to get our head around this, though, and take responsibility for fixing our training because, once we do, progress is dramatic.

Have a think about the times when your dog's obedience becomes erratic, and try to think about it in terms of your training. Focus on a task that your dog can achieve rather than on one where he fails, and try to work forwards from there in small steps.

There are three important factors to consider in any training situation:

1. **How excited is my dog?**
2. **How motivated is my dog?**
3. **How difficult is my request?**

All three interact with each other. If you are trying to teach your dog to walk to heel past other dogs, and he is leaping all over the place like a lunatic, don't allow yourself to label the dog as being disobedient. Think about how you can make it possible for him to succeed.

Reducing excitement

The best way to reduce your dog's excitement level is usually to move him farther away from the distraction. If your dog is not capable of walking to heel past your neighbour's Collie, move farther away and try again. If he cannot sit when you ask him to when someone is kicking a ball around, move him farther away, or rope in the person with the ball to help. Ask him/her to roll the ball more slowly to begin with. This isn't permanent. You won't always have to pass other dogs with a 10-metre (10-yard) clearance, but you need to find a starting point where your dog can respond to you.

Increasing motivation

Using higher-value rewards is another way to help you get past a challenging point in training. A sardine, a piece of warm roast chicken, his favourite ball; whatever your dog finds irresistible, use it. If your dog cannot sit when his favourite visitor arrives, have some warm roast meat ready. Lure the sit, and reward. Then ask for a sit, and reward. This isn't permanent. You won't need to walk around with sardines in your treat bag or have pots of chicken ready when visitors come for the next five years. You are just making it easier to get that first step right, to get to a point where the dog can break his focus on the distraction and give it back to *you*. Remember, until he has done it once (with your help), the dog doesn't know he is even capable of sitting in a situation that excites him.

Making the task easier

Sometimes the best way to cope with a challenging situation is simply to ask for an easier response. This is especially important in situations where you cannot realistically move farther away from the distraction or reduce its appeal.

Wait until the dog's ready, then reward something very simple. It could be a glance or a look in your direction, to begin with. It could progress to a hand touch, and then a sit or a few steps at heel. Again, this isn't permanent. Just another way of getting that first response on which you will be able to build. This is about training in the moment and building a history of successful responses to your cues. This kind of success quickly becomes a habit.

Regaining your dog's attention

It is much harder to control a dog that has lost his focus on you as a person. Dogs do what rewards them, and what interests them. Labradors are intelligent, co-operative, highly social dogs, with strong hunting instincts. This is why they make such outstanding gundogs. But it does mean that they function best when kept busy with some interesting teamwork. They need mental stimulation in conjunction with physical exercise. Gundog training is ideal, but there are plenty of other ways of engaging your Labrador in teamwork. The bottom line is you need to be interesting to your dog, especially outdoors, if you want to remain in control. This is particularly the case with dogs from working lines.

Manage his free time

Most young Labradors require some degree of management during a walk. Some require a great deal of management. It is a good plan to have an idea in your mind, before you set off for a walk, of just how far away from you your dog should be allowed to stray. With a youngster of six to nine months old, keep this distance very short indeed – around 20 to 30 metres (20 to 30 yards) is far enough. When your dog reaches the limit of this zone of control, call him back and reward him. Encourage him to check in of his own free will by providing valuable (to him) rewards whenever he comes back to you without being asked.

From time to time, and whenever you get bored with repeatedly calling him, bring your dog to heel and walk him along next to you for a few minutes. Spend a few minutes during each walk doing some training. Get him to sit and stay while you walk in a circle around him. Send him for that tennis ball you deliberately dropped for him a little way back. Hide behind a tree so that he has to sniff you out. Then give him a little more free time, watching all the while to make sure he does not get too far away. Best of all, every now and then, turn around and start walking back the way you came. Don't tell the dog you are about to do this, just about turn and walk the other way. Make him responsible for keeping an eye on you, and not the other way around.

As you become more interesting to your dog, and as you progress with this training, his bond with you will deepen and he will begin looking to you as a source of inspiration and fun. Once you have mastered and proofed his basic training, a world of opportunity will open up for you. A well-behaved dog can participate in many activities that will enhance both your lives. We'll be looking at putting the finishing touches to his training, and at the opportunities that will then be available to you, in Chapter 13, Advanced training, activities and sports. Right now, as those important hormones begin to shape your dog's physical and mental development, and as your dog enters the final few months of his first year, we need to look at the ins and outs of caring for a sexually mature dog.

Getting your dog's attention outside can be tricky.

12

Sexual maturity

In dogs, the production of sex hormones begins to proliferate after about six months of age, and these have a range of effects on the canine mind and body. Your dog may well be capable of breeding far sooner than you thought. So you need to be aware of your options with regard to birth control.

In this chapter, we'll take a look at the effects of sexual maturity on your dog, and at whether or not you should have him neutered. At one time, veterinary opinion was overwhelmingly against the keeping of entire dogs, and we were all recommended to have our bitches spayed and our dogs castrated. We'll look at why opinions about neutering are changing, at what that might mean for you and your Labrador, and what it is like living with an entire and sexually mature dog.

Reaching sexual maturity – your female Labrador

If you do not have her neutered, at some time, usually between six and fifteen months of age, your female Labrador will come into season. Also known as 'coming on heat', this simply means that she is entering her fertile period and will soon be ready and willing to mate with a male dog. The first indication that your bitch is coming into season is a noticeable swelling of her vulva. This is soon accompanied by bleeding from the vagina. This bloody discharge is completely normal and becomes more watery and paler as the season progresses. Some bitches have a profuse discharge and leave a trail of blood wherever they go. Others will clean themselves so scrupulously that you will hardly notice the bleeding. Your bitch's season will last up to four weeks. She is not fertile for the entire period, but it is best to assume that she is. The chances of pregnancy are highest towards the middle of the season, as the bleeding starts to tail off, but there is no safe time when you can leave a female on heat unsupervised in the vicinity of entire male dogs. This means you will need to change your behaviour during this time in order to make sure your bitch does not become pregnant.

A bitch on heat gives off powerful pheromones that entire male dogs find incredibly attractive. They can smell these pheromones from far away. Therefore, you should not walk an in-season bitch in public places or leave her unsupervised in a garden or yard that is not absolutely secure. Hedges and low fences will not prevent a male dog getting into your property at this time, and some in-season bitches will attempt to escape from their garden by jumping over or digging under fences, even if this is not normal behaviour for them at other times.

Birth control is the responsibility of the bitch owner, and it is especially important because there is no *safe* morning-after or abortion treatment for dogs. Drugs that terminate pregnancy in dogs have significant risks attached to them. The only safe and sensible way to ensure your fertile bitch does not get pregnant is to prevent access to her by male dogs. This usually means keeping her at home, in a secure garden, for about four weeks. No harm will come to your bitch from not being taken for a walk during this time.

Some bitches show changes in temperament during their season, becoming a little more clingy, for example. Many in-season bitches will mount or hump other dogs or bitches when they are on heat. Your bitch will also need to urinate more often while she is in season and accidents are not uncommon at this time. These changes are temporary and revert once the season is over. From now on, your bitch will probably come on heat every six months or so for the rest of her life, or until she is spayed.

Pyometra

Once your Labrador has completed her first season and is back to normal, she needs to be put on pyometra watch for the next few weeks. Pyometra is an infection of the uterus or womb, and therefore, cannot affect a male dog, or a female dog that has had her uterus removed. However, if you have an unspayed bitch, you should make sure you know a little bit about this very common and potentially fatal disease, especially the symptoms.

A Swedish study showed that around 24 per cent of all unspayed female dogs will get pyometra, which is a little like appendicitis in that the uterus becomes inflamed, infected and filled with pus. But the uterus is a *much* bigger organ than the appendix, and may even swell sufficiently for your dog to look pregnant. If pyometra goes untreated, the uterus may eventually rupture and the dog will die. The risk of contracting pyometra increases with each season that the dog has. So although young dogs do occasionally get it, older dogs are much more at risk than younger ones.

There are two types of pyometra – open and closed. This refers to the cervix (neck of the womb). Closed pyometra is more dangerous than open pyometra, simply because it is harder to detect. With open pyometra, pus will drain from the vagina and will usually be noticed by the dog's owner.

It is not always easy to tell that your bitch has pyometra. Dogs are tough creatures and quite good at concealing pain or unpleasant symptoms. A slight vaginal discharge may be quickly cleaned up by your bitch and with closed pyometra there will be no discharge at all. The best way to keep your intact bitch safe is to observe her carefully. For one to two months after each season, look out for reduced appetite, general malaise and an increased thirst, with or without vaginal discharge. Have your Labrador bitch checked by your vet if you see any of these signs. Vaginal discharge in any intact bitch outside her season is a cause for concern, no matter how well she seems. It warrants a *same-day* appointment with your vet. Speed is of the utmost importance, potentially a life saver.

Pyometra is usually treated with emergency surgery. The area around the swollen, infected uterus is packed to avoid contaminating other organs and the uterus is carefully removed through a large incision in your dog's belly. This is a much more difficult and hazardous operation than an elective spay, and paying for it will make a significant dent in your wallet. Spaying will prevent your bitch from getting pyometra.

False pregnancy

At the end of each season, some female Labradors will develop a condition commonly known as false or phantom pregnancy. There will be changes in her body that would have taken place if she had been pregnant. This may include some swelling of the mammary tissue and actual production of fluid, which may leak from her nipples. It may also include changes in behaviour. She may start nest-building, collecting toys or items of clothing and arranging them in her basket. She may become clingy, or lose her appetite. Like pyometra, these changes are triggered by hormones and tend to occur a month or so after the end of a season. Some bitches have increasingly severe symptoms with increasing age. Contact your vet if you

think your bitch is having a phantom pregnancy. If symptoms are significant, he may recommend treating her with hormones, and you may want to consider having her spayed to prevent a recurrence.

Reaching sexual maturity – your male Labrador

Once your male Labrador reaches six months of age, the amount of testosterone in his bloodstream begins to increase rapidly. Like females, the male dog is sexually mature and capable of breeding long before he is emotionally mature or even fully grown. At some point towards the end of the first year, or soon afterwards, most male dogs begin to cock their legs when urinating rather than squatting like a bitch. This simply enables the dog to leave his scent on raised objects and vegetation in order to announce his presence to other dogs, and it's a sign that he is growing up.

Humping
Some sexually mature male dogs will sometimes masturbate by humping inanimate objects, such as blankets or toys, or by humping people or other dogs. Humping is also a fairly common behaviour in younger puppies and in dogs of both sexes, although it is not sexual in this context. With some adult dogs, humping can become a rather embarrassing habit but, for most adult males, this is *not* the case. The best way to deal with casual humping is to distract the dog and keep him occupied. If you let it become a habit, it may persist, even after neutering.

Independence
Once your dog's testosterone kicks in, he will probably become more confident and independent. We looked at how this can affect your relationship in Chapter 11, Growing up and adolescence. Your entire male will also become very interested in female dogs that are in season. This is the point at which some young male dogs begin to test the boundaries of their premises, jumping gates and fences in order to pursue their love lives.

People sometimes worry that an entire male will get into fights, but most Labradors get along well with other dogs of either sex. However, in the UK, many vets recommend that all male dogs be neutered, and it is important that you know the pros and cons of this process before you arrange to whip away your dog's reproductive equipment. So let's move on and take a look at neutering.

🐾 The effects of neutering

Neutering involves removing the organs responsible for producing sex hormones. One of the problems with this procedure is that sex hormones are not just responsible for sexual maturation and sexual behaviour; they have other important roles to play. We are now beginning to understand that sex hormones in dogs have a much wider influence on their various organ systems, and that the effects of neutering are more far reaching than once thought.

The operations

Neutering female dogs can be a major operation, which leaves a large central wound in the belly, and it takes the bitch a couple of weeks to recover. More recently, a laparoscopic spay has been introduced, which simply removes the ovaries via a small incision. This is a less invasive procedure but is slightly more expensive than a traditional spay due to the special equipment required.

Neutering a male dog is a much simpler procedure. The testes are removed through a small incision in the scrotum.

If you have your female dog neutered, she will no longer come into season, or be able to have puppies. If you have your male dog castrated, he will gradually lose interest in mating and, a short time after neutering, he will become infertile. Countries vary with regard to the age at which these procedures are commonly carried out. Early neutering (before six months) is common in the USA, while in the UK, many dogs are neutered towards the end of their first year. In some countries, neutering is not normally carried out on healthy dogs at all.

The rationale

The reasons why people have these procedures carried out on their dogs are varied. In many cases, birth control is the main one, or they are simply following mainstream veterinary advice. But the underlying reasons for opting for, or agreeing to, neutering sometimes lie in misconceptions people have about how the operation will change their dog's behaviour, or impact on his health.

Neutering a bitch is often done for the sake of convenience. If your bitch is neutered, you will no longer have to worry about keeping her home for at least three weeks twice a year, ensuring that she does not come into contact with any male dogs, or keeping her off your cream carpets. These reasons are neither right nor wrong. They are simply the choices that people make. But it is important that those making these choices are aware of the implications of their decision.

The truth is that neutering may change your dog in ways you do not expect, and may not change him at all in ways you do expect. People often hope and expect that their male dog will be easier to manage after castration, and they may be disappointed. Many of the changes that can occur after castration, occur only in some castrated dogs. The success rate of castration in curing a whole range of perceived problems is not very impressive.

Appearance and sexual behaviour

Here are some of the things that might happen if you have your male puppy castrated. He is unlikely to develop in quite the same way as an entire male. He may, in fact, look a little feminine. He may also grow a little taller than he would have done if you had left him intact. This is because testosterone is involved in the cessation of bone growth. Constant scent marking – cocking his leg every five minutes – may be reduced in castrated males, but there are no guarantees. Humping may be less likely to become an issue in neutered males if the dog is castrated before it becomes a habit. On the other hand, humping is not a problem in most entire males, either. With bitches, the most significant difference in appearance after spaying is often poorer coat condition.

Boisterous behaviour and roaming

Bouncy, lively and generally boisterous behaviour is unlikely to be reduced as a result of neutering, in either male or female Labradors. Boisterous adolescence is normal. Labradors may become calmer as they mature, but don't assume this is down to neutering.

Roaming is one behaviour that is significantly improved after castration, because roaming in males tends to be powered by the testosterone that drives the urge to procreate. In bitches, the desire to roam is *mostly* confined to periods during which the bitch is in season. However, operating on your dog is not necessary in order to prevent roaming. Secure fencing will perform the same function, and also help keep your dog safe from accidents. Obviously, if your garden is the size of a football pitch, that could work out expensive, and a smaller enclosure for your dog might be an alternative solution.

Aggression and fighting

People sometimes worry that intact male dogs will become aggressive or dominant, and so opt for neutering. However, the vast majority of entire male Labradors are peaceful and friendly. It is also worth considering that aggression in dogs is frequently triggered by fear, and testosterone is a confidence-building hormone. So neutering your male Labrador if he is a little nervous or sensitive *could* make things worse.

Health benefits and risks

When it comes to health, there are both benefits and risks to neutering. Until recently, it was widely considered to be an entirely beneficial procedure. We now know that this is not the case. The situation is far more complex and the benefits need to be considered against the risks.

The health benefits of neutering a male dog include removing the risk of testicular cancer, and a reduction in prostate problems (not cancers) in older dogs. Neutering your bitch will prevent her from contracting pyometra, a common infection of the womb, which we discussed earlier in this chapter. Neutering a bitch before her first season will remove her risk of mammary cancer almost entirely. Neutering after the second season will significantly reduce this risk.

However, this is not such good news as it might at first appear. Sadly, there is a growing body of evidence to suggest that both spayed bitches and castrated dogs are at significantly greater risk of *other* cancers. A study of Hungarian Vizslas born between 1992 and 2008 showed that neutered Viszlas were much more likely to get a whole range of cancers than dogs that were not neutered. This applied to both males and females. A study of Golden Retrievers published in 2013 looked at the relationship between neutering and both hip dysplasia and cancer. It showed an increased risk of joint problems in neutered dogs, and again, it showed a link between neutering and a significantly increased risk of several cancers. A follow-up study comparing Labradors with Goldens suggests that the risk of neutering in Labradors may be lower than in Golden Retrievers, but the situation is far from clear-cut.

A US study comparing life expectancy between neutered dogs and entire dogs also showed that, overall, more neutered dogs died from cancer than intact dogs. Despite this, the study also showed a greater longevity in neutered dogs, which seemed less prone to accidents. However, because neutering in the USA is generally accepted as the responsible way to behave, it is difficult to compare the two groups. In fact, the main causes of death in the intact dogs in this study were disease and accidents, both of which are largely preventable by good veterinary care (vaccinations) and management (preventing roaming). This could simply be a reflection of the ownership styles of the two different groups. Cancers are not the only issue. Another study showed that neutered dogs are more likely to suffer from age-related cognitive impairment, rather like dementia in people, than their entire friends. And we know that neutered bitches, especially in larger breeds, are more likely to suffer from incontinence than bitches that retain their ovaries and, therefore, their oestrogen supply. Spay incontinence may be treatable in some cases.

Whether or not you choose to neuter your dog may depend on whether or not the dog is male or female. There is no doubt that pyometra is a serious risk for female dogs, especially as they get older. You may feel that neutering in middle age will help to keep her safe from this disease while avoiding some of the disadvantages of early neutering. After two of my spaniels contracted pyometra, I had my healthy middle-aged spaniel neutered to protect her. However, in the light of the latest research on cancer, I am holding off on that decision for my two Labradors. It isn't an easy choice.

For males, neutering is not such an invasive operation, but there does seem to be less overall benefit. Obviously, castrating a dog will render him infertile (although not immediately), which may be very important to you if you own, or are intending to own, an entire bitch. If you have a dog and a bitch, neutering the dog is probably the least invasive option. If your dog is an only dog, well socialised and bred from parents with a great temperament, and if your property

There are pros and cons to neutering.

is secure, castrating your dog is not necessarily the best thing for him. It depends very much on what you are trying to achieve. One recent development for male dogs being castrated for behavioural reasons is chemical castration. This might be something you could try on a temporary basis, to see if it has the desired effect, before resorting to the more permanent solution.

Do talk to your vet about your concerns. Ask about the most recent research – he/she will probably have read the recent studies and will have an opinion on what this means for you and your dog. If your vet isn't abreast of the research on neutering, get a second opinion. It's definitely worth taking some time to do your own research before you remove parts of your Labrador. After all, you can't put them back again, and you don't want to make a decision that you may later come to regret.

 ## SUMMARY

Sexual maturity is a normal and natural part of a young Labrador's life, and for many Labradors has little in the way of adverse effects. Some Labrador owners will struggle a little with teenage behaviour, but this is the case with neutered dogs, too. It is not true that entire adult males all fight, or hump everything that moves; nor is it true that neutering is necessarily in the best interests of an adult male's health. There are many, many entire male Labradors living useful and happy lives, so don't be pressured into neutering your boy if you don't want to.

For bitches, the risks of being left entire are significant, especially with advancing age. Whether or not these risks outweigh the risks of cancer and the joint issues associated with neutering is not clear. Up to a quarter of entire bitches will get pyometra. On the other hand, a significant proportion of spayed bitches may get cancer as a result of being neutered. No one has all the answers and, ultimately, this is a decision you will have to make yourself, hopefully with some considered input from your vet.

If you decide to leave your dog or bitch entire, there may come a time when you look at your beautiful adult dog and ask yourself, 'Wouldn't it be nice to have puppies?' It is a very natural thing to want to add to your canine family with a puppy that is a son or daughter of the dog you love. That is the subject of Chapter 14, Breeding from your Labrador.

Since there are a great many Labradors in the world, and because it is a responsible thing to do, many people will breed only from Labradors that have a particular talent, either in the field, as a working gundog or in working trials, or in the show ring. So before we move onto breeding, we're going to have a look at some of the sports and activities that are open to your dog once he is mature and has some basic training under his belt.

13

Advanced training, activities and sports

cannot write about the world's most talented dog without taking a look at the ways in which you could enhance your dog's natural abilities, and the many and varied activities you could enjoy together. The operative word here is 'could' not 'should'. Every Labrador ever born has a huge amount of potential, and, in many cases, this potential remains untapped throughout the life of the dog. People sometimes say to me, 'Is it wrong to keep a retriever and never work him?' They worry that the dog will be unhappy if he doesn't get a chance to work on a shoot or compete in the show ring. This is especially the case when

Clever dogs love advanced training.

the dog is from working lines. I hope I can put your mind at rest on this one. Provided that you and your dog are both enjoying life, it doesn't matter one bit whether or not he gets a chance to be a working gundog, shine on the agility circuit or win trophies in an arena. He doesn't know what he is missing, nor does he care, and neither should you. What matters to him is your company, your kindness, food, exercise, fresh air and fun.

If your dog enjoys long daily walks with his family, and a happy, relaxed home environment, he won't be pining for what might have been. But if the idea of challenging your dog, getting him fitter, teaching him to retrieve, jump obstacles, follow hand signals, find hidden objects or follow scent trails appeals to you, then you might very well enjoy the chance to get involved with some kind of sporting activity or specialised training. It isn't just gundog work that your dog might enjoy, although we will look at that in more detail in a moment. You have a wide variety of sports and activities open to you. From simply accompanying you on long runs or hikes, to learning to work as a team together, the Labrador is one of the most versatile and successful canine athletes in the world. So, if you can do it, and it doesn't require wheels or opposable thumbs, he can probably do it, too!

Running with your Labrador

Probably the simplest sporting activity you can share with your Labrador is running. If you enjoy pulling on some trainers and taking off in the fresh air, you can certainly enjoy it even more with your four-legged companion. Once your adult Labrador's joints are mature, he can accompany you on increasingly long runs. You do need to take a number of safety precautions, even with a fit breed such as this one. Build up stamina and endurance gradually, just as you do for yourself. If you plunge straight in with an unfit dog, you are going to have muscle damage and possibly worse. Long-distance running, especially on hard surfaces, can give dogs very sore paws if they are not acclimatised gradually. So take it step by step. If you are going to start running with an older dog, take him to the vet for a health check, first. If you are a serious marathon runner, this is a must for a dog of any age. Make sure you don't run your dog too hard in warm weather – early morning and evening are best, and make sure he is well hydrated. Heatstroke is a very serious matter, so if you are running during the heat of the day, leave your friend at home. Never be tempted to clip or shave a Labrador to keep him cool – he will get sunburnt.

In some areas, you can participate in Canicross, which is a running sport specifically designed for dogs and their owners. The dogs wear a special harness and must remain attached to their owner at all times. You can find the Canicross website for the UK listed at the back of this book. Events take place in a range of different locations.

Arena sports

This covers activities that take place within a relatively confined area. They usually involve a degree of competition, and follow a strict set of rules with which you'll need to become acquainted. You have to belong to a club to take part in most of them, but they are enormous fun, and a great way to make friends with other Labrador owners. Some of these activities are arranged by the Kennel Club, some by independent organisations. You'll find contact details for these in the back of this book. If you want to get involved in gundog fieldwork, it is best to avoid activities that encourage your dog to make a noise. Otherwise, if your dog is full-grown and in good health, dive straight in!

Flyball

Noisy, fast, exciting and fun – if that sounds appealing, flyball might be the sport for you. The canine flyball competitor has to run up a track, over a series of small jumps, catch/collect a ball, and run back again. Dogs compete in relay teams and are categorised by size. This is a great sport for ball-crazy Labradors, run by national Flyball Associations.

Agility is great exercise and will strengthen your bond.

Agility

Weaving in and out of brightly coloured poles, racing through tunnels and balancing on see-saws – this is the sport of agility. It's a very exciting and often noisy activity that tests the speed, balance and, of course, agility of each dog over a specially designed obstacle course. When we think of agility work, we often associate this with small to medium breeds but a Labrador can excel. The smaller, lighter strains of working-bred Labradors seem to be particularly well suited to these competitions. Check the Dog Agility Association for more information.

Competitive obedience

If you have mastered some basic obedience at home with your Labrador, you might be interested in joining a dog-training club and having a go at competitive obedience tests. There are six levels of formal obedience test in the UK, and dogs can start competing at six months of age. Dogs are tested over a range of tasks, including heelwork, recall, stay and, at advanced levels, distance control and directions. Tests take place at obedience shows around the country in the form of competitions rather than assessments. So whether or not you win or lose depends to an extent on whom you are up against on the day. Obedience competitions and trials are held under the auspices of the Kennel Club and competing is a lot of fun and a great way to ensure your dog gets trained to the highest standards.

Heelwork to music

This has been around for a few years now, and is often the subject of entries in popular talent competitions. It is essentially an obedience routine set to music. A spin-off, known as Freestyle, involves the more exciting and complex moves you've probably seen on YouTube or television.

Collies are the most popular breed for this sport but Labradors do well at it, too, and if you enjoy training, you'll probably enjoy learning new routines and setting them to music. You'll be able to find out more from your local obedience club.

Dock diving

This is a relatively new craze, where dogs leap into a specially constructed pool. The longest/highest jumps are measured and Labradors – the ultimate water dogs – often excel. Dock diving is well established in the USA and is becoming popular in the UK.

If your Labrador is not yet confident in the water, look at Chapter 8, Daily care of your Labrador, for ways to get him swimming competently.

Pets As Therapy

Up and down the country, hundreds of Labradors and their owners are helping to make the world a nicer place for people who are lonely, isolated or unwell. These dogs are organised by a charity called Pets As Therapy, and adult Labradors are often well suited to this valuable work.

Pets As Therapy, or PAT-dogs as they are often known, accompany their owners into nursing homes, children's homes and hospitals, or on visits to vulnerable people who live alone and are in need of support and company. Working with a PAT dog is a wonderful way of making a difference to people's lives. The dogs must be calm and past the boisterous stage, and free from any kind of aggression or nervousness. Many well-behaved Labradors over two or three years of age are suitable for PAT-dog work. All you need is a willingness to go through the induction process, and to give up a little of your spare time to help others.

Pets As Therapy Dogs is a national charity founded in 1983. At the time of writing, there are around four and a half thousand PAT dogs registered with the charity, and over a hundred cats. Between them, they visit over a hundred and thirty thousand people every week! You can find more information on how to enroll your dog as a PAT-dog on the Pets As Therapy website, listed at the end of this book.

Teaching more advanced skills

In Chapter 11, Growing up and adolescence, we looked at establishing some basic obedience skills, including walking on a loose lead, coming when called and the sit/stay, and we looked at how to advance those skills by teaching your dog to obey your cues under distraction. Some interesting new skills are required for your dog to participate in a number of sports and activities. A lot of fun is to be had in teaching your dog the send away and remote stop, or training him to follow a scent trail or hand signals at a distance, to jump obstacles or deliver a ball into your hand.

Mastering these kinds of skills often takes place in a training group or class. Much of it can be done at home, though, if you are familiar with the principles of training and have some basic skill in luring and shaping. What follows is a brief summary to give you an idea of where to begin, and how to progress.

Whatever you want to teach your dog, focus on the principles of training. Dogs do what works for them, and to train a dog, you must provide motivation for the dog to engage in the activity of your choice. For new or complicated activities, shape or lure the new behaviour first, then give it a name.

Send away

There are several different ways to teach a send away, which is when the dog runs away from you in a straight line. Gundogs are traditionally taught the send-away, or 'back', command using retrieves. The main drawback of this method is that it is limited to an extent by the dog's enthusiasm for retrieving. If your dog is a keen retriever, you can certainly try it. You'll find full instructions in the Gundog Club's Grade Three retriever training manual and on my Totally Gundogs website, where it is called 'lining'.

Obedience trainers teach the dog to run to a mat or to run around a pole or cone. The 'run around' is a great method, suitable for all dogs. You'll need a portable object or marker, such as a cone, for the dog to go around. Start indoors in a small quiet room and lure or shape the dog to go around the marker. If you are luring, remember to lose the lure quickly and replace with a hand signal. Once he is willingly going around the marker, you can start to place it farther away, so that he has to travel away from you, around the marker, then back again to get his reward. Remember to reduce the distances right back to zero when starting to proof in new locations or in the presence of distractions.

Remote stop

Partnered with the send away is the remote stop. After all, you don't want the dog to simply keep going forever. So the remote stop provides limits to the send away and enables you to lose the mat or marker that he was aiming for. In gundog work, the remote stop is an essential part of directional control.

There are many different ways to teach and practise the remote stop, but, like so many skills, the secret is to get it right at short distances and then gradually increase the space between you and your dog. You can start at home, in your kitchen. If you ask your dog to sit as he is moving towards you, initially, he will probably not sit until he reaches you. But if every time you do this, you throw a treat behind him, over his head, he will soon start to sit as soon as he hears your cue. If you have baby gates in your house, you can reinforce sits on the other side of the gate. Stand right next to the gate to start with, you on one side and the dog on the other, then capture or lure a sit. Once he has caught onto your game, take a step back from the gate and repeat. Keep building up the distance. Once you take this game into the garden, you'll need to reward your dog by throwing him a ball or toy because it is hard for him to find food on the ground. You can also attach him to your fence or a tree, using a harness and lead. Stand right in front of him to begin with and move farther away only when he sits quickly on your cue. Click each sit and return to the dog to give him his treat.

Directional control

It is fascinating to watch a dog being controlled and directed at a distance. If you have ever watched a sheepdog or a gundog working in partnership with his handler, who uses a range of whistles and hand signals, you will know how complicated it looks. Actually, it isn't as hard to teach as you might think. A

gundog's motivation to respond and earn his reward is the retrieve. Any Labrador that loves to retrieve can be taught to follow hand signals at a distance. Dogs have evolved an instinctive understanding of human body language, so introducing simple hand signals is not difficult. The secret is to start close up, and add the distances later. A training lead can be used to prevent the dog rewarding himself for going the wrong way. Full directional control is achieved using a combination of send aways, remote stops and casting, which simply means sending the dog in different directions using hand signals. You can find detailed instructions for teaching and practising directional control on my Totally Gundogs website.

Complex retrieves take time and dedication.

Jumping

Many dog sports involve jumping, and teaching your dog to jump is fun. You'll need a jump that can be raised in stages, so that your dog can build up his confidence with easy jumps before moving onto more challenging ones. It is a good idea to wait until the dog has finished growing before doing much in the way of jumping, in order to reduce the risk of damage to the growth plates in his joints.

You can buy agility-style jumps fairly cheaply and these are light, portable and easy to set up. Set the

Working Labradors need to learn to jump high obstacles safely.

jump just an inch or two off the ground and lure or lead the dog over it, reinforcing each time with a marker sound and a treat. Get the dog jumping of his own free will before even thinking about a cue. Associate the cue word of your choice (I use 'Over') for a few sessions, and then begin raising the height of the jump. If you raise it too fast, the dog will try to go under when it gets high enough. So take your time.

Retrieving to hand

A retrieve can be anything from grabbing a tennis ball and dropping it at your feet, to a long and complicated endeavour involving a previously hidden item that the dog has to be guided towards using directional control. This is your Labrador's true purpose.

One of the key components of the retrieve is the delivery to hand, especially if you plan to take part in the advanced sports we are going to discuss in a moment. The importance of placing the retrieve directly into your hand derives from the Labrador's role in returning wounded game to his handler. If he dropped a wounded bird or animal on the ground, it might get up and run away. So delivery to hand is essential for a working gundog. It is often a sticking point for pet Labrador owners, but is quite easy to fix using a clicker-trained retrieve.

The clicker retrieve teaches the dog to pick up and hold an item in his mouth and then to place that item in his owner's hand. Again, you can find full instructions for teaching this skill on my Totally Gundogs website.

Coping with challenges

If you are struggling with advanced training, remember that there is always a solution. Do one of the following:

- **Raise the value of your rewards.**
- **Give treats more frequently.**
- **Dilute the distraction.**
- **Ask for a less demanding response.**

This is not cheating, bribery, relying on food or any of the other myths that you will hear from people not well acquainted with behavioural science. It is simply a way of establishing this *new* behaviour. Going back to treat streaming (see Chapter 9, Principles of Labrador training) will often get you out of a rut. Once your dog is competent, you can fade the treats so that you are reinforcing chains or sequences of behaviour, or longer periods of sustained behaviour, and you can reduce the value of the treats.

Diluting distractions means putting more distance between your dog and the distraction. If that is not possible, ask your dog to do something less challenging. The aim is for him to focus on you, and work with you. Then you can gradually ask for more.

Remember, no dog is going to cope with huge distractions without this kind of preparation. You have to fake it to make it! You can find many more examples of how to set up these training scenarios in my book, *Total Recall*.

Advanced sports

If you fancy more of a challenge, you might like to consider two wonderful outdoor sports at which Labradors excel. Anyone can take part. The first is working trials, and the second is, of course, the Labrador's *raison d'etre*, gundog fieldwork and the competitions associated with it.

Advanced sports can be challenging and very rewarding.

Working trials

Based on military and police-dog training practices, working trials involve a combination of physical agility and strength, obedience, and great tracking and retrieving skills. Dogs have to learn to complete long jumps, high jumps, retrieves, send aways, tracking-scent trails and more. Labradors lead the way in this great sport, and there are a series of levels of difficulty and awards that you can work towards. Working trials are governed by the Kennel Club and you can get involved through your local Working Trials Society. You'll find a list of these and more information on the Kennel Club website.

There are plenty of activities that Labradors excel at.

Gundog fieldwork

Gundog work is where the Labrador Retriever excels. Before your dog can participate, he needs to be trained to a reasonable standard and introduced to gunfire and game under controlled conditions. The Gundog Club has a network of accredited instructors throughout the UK who can assist you with this, and the club provides a graded training system with Field Test assessments to help you and your dog progress in achievable stages. In the USA, you will need to join your local retriever training club, where you will be able to work through the

Hunt Test grading schemes provided by the AKC and UKC.

You need to be aware that gundog work is one of the last dog sports and disciplines that has not yet widely adopted modern dog-training methods. In the UK, this means that some gundog handlers do still rely to some extent on aversives, especially when proofing against distractions. In the USA, where electric collars have been widely adopted by the retriever-training community, a great deal of training is carried out using punishment as the primary motivator. So it is a good idea, if you want to train your Labrador *without* aversives, to make sure your basic training is well established with some proofing under way in advance of joining a gundog-training group or class. That way, you can learn the practical skills involved while using your own training style and methods.

Once your dog is experienced in the field, there are opportunities to compete against other trained dogs through entering gundog Field Trials put on by the Kennel Club.

SUMMARY

Labradors love nothing more than to be busy. They have tremendous physical and mental potential and, if you like the idea of taking your training to a new level, your dog will love joining in. Without doubt, the activity most suited to these amazing dogs is the one for which their ancestors were bred.

Even if you don't like the idea of hunting and shooting, you can participate in gundog-style training. There is no more exhilarating sight than a powerful Labrador flying across a field, leaping a fence, swimming a stream, collecting a dummy and then flying back to his handler with not a moment's hesitation. All Labradors benefit from being taught gundog skills. Retriever training harnesses their natural instincts, deepens the bond between each dog and his handler and prevents boredom and naughtiness. One of the aims of the Gundog Club is to open up opportunities for pet Labradors to participate in these exciting activities through the Graded Training Scheme.

Advanced training and joining in a sport or activity tailor made for your dog is a hugely rewarding experience, and takes just a little investment of your time. You never know, you might have a star in the making.

If your dog turns out to be especially talented, your thoughts might turn to breeding. That is the topic of the next chapter. We'll be taking a look at the risks and benefits of breeding from you dog, and at the moral and financial implications. Let's find out what's involved.

14

Breeding from your Labrador

Y ou would not be the first Labrador owner to look at your handsome boy or beautiful girl and feel a rush of longing to have another just like your lovely dog. What could be more wonderful or more natural?

This chapter is not intended to teach you how to become a Labrador breeder, but rather to give you a flavour of what is involved, and to help you decide if breeding is really for you. We'll be taking a look at the various reasons people decide to breed from their dogs, and at the health risks and financial costs involved. This may seem a little negative initially, but breeding is not for the faint hearted, so it's a good idea to be clear about what you are getting yourself into. If you think breeding is an adventure you would like to embark on, then it is important that you have the right dog or dogs to breed from. So we'll be taking a look at the principles of responsible breeding and what prospective buyers are looking for when they search for a puppy to bring into their lives.

Why do people breed from their dogs?

The idea that every bitch should have a litter before being spayed, for her own sake, was once common. If you were under the impression that it would do your bitch good to have a litter, then you can relax. This really is an old wives' tale, rather like the belief that having a litter will settle down an excitable bitch. There is no truth in either of these myths. There are no health benefits to a bitch experiencing pregnancy in advance of being spayed, and excitable bitches are no less excitable as a result of becoming mothers. The only likely outcome is a litter of equally excitable puppies. Nor is there any certainty that your own dog's appearance or temperament will materialise in his or her progeny. Your puppy could turn out much more like dad than like mum, or vice versa.

Tiny puppies and their mother need a lot of care and attention.

To make money

I'm not going to get into the moral issues that surround breeding dogs for money, because it is a very subjective topic. However, in practical terms, there is rarely any profit in breeding a single litter from your bitch, or in standing your dog at stud on a single occasion. This is because the cost of the health tests involved outweigh the profit on all but the largest litter. We'll look at those costs in a bit more detail in a moment.

For the children

It is possible that breeding a litter will be a good experience for your children. But where a family pet is concerned, there is huge scope for things to go badly wrong (see risks below). While there is undoubtedly pleasure to be had for all the family with an easy, uncomplicated litter, it is a significant gamble to take.

The risks to your bitch

Most births are straightforward, but a fair proportion are not. One study found that over 60 per cent of bitches that experience birthing problems need a Caesarian section. The study also showed that around five in every one thousand bitches get into trouble during labour. So while the risks are not huge, they are not small, either. It could happen to your dog. Bear in mind also that stillborn puppies are a relatively common occurrence in any Labrador birth, and that it is not unusual for one or more puppies to be sickly and need extra care and veterinary attention.

The risks to your bitch do not end once the birth is over. Post-partum infection or haemorrhage is a possibility. Mastitis or infection of the milk ducts may occur. With a large litter of strong-suckling puppies, it is not unusual for the bitch to suffer from milk fever or eclampsia. This is caused by the sudden depletion of the mother's calcium reserves as she provides for the puppies faster than her body can replenish her blood calcium levels. Milk fever can come on quite rapidly, and is most likely to occur two to three weeks after the birth. It is a medical emergency and needs immediate veterinary attention.

The risks to your dog

Although he does not have to endure pregnancy, mating is not risk free for your male dog, either. It is not uncommon for a stud dog to be injured during the mating process. The male dog has a bone in his penis and this may be damaged. The risks can be reduced by experienced handling, especially during the tie – the period of time after ejaculation when the male is unable to remove his penis from the female dog's vagina.

Some dogs behave differently after being mated. They become more interested in bitches generally, more inclined to try to escape from your property or to roam if not closely supervised. Some may get very distressed if a neighbour's dog comes on heat. This is something you do need to consider.

The challenges of breeding

It goes without saying that being involved in the creation of a new generation of Labradors is a big responsibility. Very real challenges are involved, too, not least of which is what it will cost you.

Financial cost

Pre-breeding health tests are expensive and you will also need to buy certain equipment and services (see below) if you intend raising a litter.

- Stud fee
- Worming and veterinary antenatal care
- Extra food for pregnant and lactating bitch
- Whelping box, heat pads and vetbedding
- Worming medicines for puppies
- Kennel Club registration
- Food for weaning
- Puppy pen
- Advertising costs
- First vaccinations and vet checks
- Costs of extra care and vaccinations for any pups unsold after eight weeks

As the bitch owner, it is vital that you also have a fund available to pay for medical treatment, including an emergency Caesarian section should she need one to save her life. Check with your vet how much you need to put by. It is unlikely that bills arising from pregnancy or birth will be covered by your insurance policy.

Time and loss of sleep and income

A pregnant bitch requires your absolute and undivided attention from the moment she goes into labour until several hours after her last puppy has arrived safely. This whole process can take twenty-four hours or more. That means no sleep for you. After that time, a responsible adult must be on your premises and available to see to your bitch's needs, and those of her puppies, for the next seven to eight weeks. Making sure the puppies are clean, fed and generally well-cared for is enormously time-consuming. You cannot hold down a full-time job and breed a litter at the same time, unless either your boss is willing to give you six weeks off, or you have another adult available to replace you at home. If you have to hand-rear the puppies due to a problem with your bitch, you will need to feed every two hours to begin with, so you'll need another adult on hand so that you can work in shifts.

Mess

Most bitches make a pretty good job of cleaning up after their pups until you start to wean them after about three weeks. If all has gone very well, then for the first three weeks you will be able to gaze at this adorable pile of Labrador loveliness with a deep sense of pleasure. Everything changes at weaning time.

From this time onwards, feeding and cleaning up is your job. Bear in mind that all puppies have the primary objective of covering themselves in poo during their every waking moment. As fast as you clean them up, they will get messy again. This process is no fun at all, and the bigger and livelier the puppies get, the more challenging the cleaning process becomes. You will need the biggest mountain of newspaper in history, and a lot of warm soapy water and patience. The cleaning-up process takes place every time you feed (six times daily), and in-between when necessary. This is hard and smelly work, especially with kibble-fed puppies.

Breeding Labradors is a serious responsibility.

Worry and intrusion

As a bitch owner, perhaps the biggest challenge of all is finding excellent homes for the beautiful puppies you have been instrumental in producing. You will need to interview your prospective puppy owners to make sure that they are suitably equipped to raise and care for a Labrador. This can be a stressful experience, especially if sufficient homes fail to materialise once the puppies are over eight weeks old.

You will need to host visits to your litter, which can be an intrusive and, especially with a large litter, time-consuming exercise. Some families will outstay their welcome and try your patience. Once the puppies have gone to their new homes, you will need to provide back-up and support, and be ready to answer lots of questions, often at quite unsociable hours. This is all part of being a responsible breeder.

With each day that passes after nine or ten weeks, puppies become a little less puppyish. Many puppy buyers don't want to miss out on those early weeks and older puppies can be harder to home. It is therefore important that you find homes for your litter without delay. The best way to do this is to make sure you have bred responsibly from the right dogs, and can fulfil the requirements of today's choosy and increasingly well-informed puppy buyers. Let's take a look now at the kind of dog you need to own before you can reasonably consider breeding from him or her.

The ideal breeding dog

When we set about breeding a litter, it is tempting to think about what we want in a puppy, but the truth is, it isn't necessarily just what *you* want that matters. Even if you are keeping a pup for yourself, the majority of your litter will need new homes. It is therefore what the puppy-buying public want from a puppy that you should be considering. They are looking for excellence in three categories: temperament, health and achievements.

Temperament

Labradors are renowned for their good temperament, but not all Labradors are perfect in this respect. Is your dog openly friendly to all and sundry, from toddlers to old folk, male or female? Is he/she confident and fearless, as comfortable in a busy town centre as in the countryside? These are essential features of a prospective Labrador parent.

Health

Is your Labrador fully mature, fit and brimming with health? Most importantly, has he/she passed with flying colours the important health tests required for Labradors? You'll find more details on those below. Puppy buyers will want to see health-test certificates for both bitch and stud dog.

Many people deciding to breed are ready to meet these health and temperament criteria, but far fewer have given much consideration to the third important feature of a quality breeding bitch or stud dog.

Achievements

Consider why a perfect stranger looking for a puppy should chose your bitch's litter over all the other bitches having litters this year, or why a bitch owner investing a substantial amount of money in a litter should pick your dog as a stud.

Perhaps your girl or boy has been placed in a few Field Trials or working tests, or is an outstanding working gundog? Maybe he or she is an agility champion? Has your dog won several major awards in the show ring? Do you have some obedience or working trials trophies on your sideboard? The point is, your dog needs some measurable quality that places him or her above all the other pets out there that are making puppies.

Many puppy buyers will be happy if the mother of their puppy has *parents* that have distinguished themselves, even if the bitch herself has not won any award. With the stud dog, people often expect more in the way of achievements. After all, one stud dog can service a lot of bitches, and successful stud dogs are available to almost anyone who has a health-tested bitch (and, sadly, sometimes to those who have not bothered with tests). For the price of a puppy, your next-door neighbour can probably have her dog mated by a top field-trial champion, or the winner of best in show at Crufts. So you need to ask yourself why would she choose *your* dog as a stud, or why a puppy buyer would want one of his puppies. This is an important consideration if you want to get your own boy mated.

Health testing

Most people would agree that responsible breeding is something we should all be aiming to encourage and promote, for the welfare of both the dogs being bred from, and for future generations of Labradors. One of the more important aspects of responsible breeding is ensuring the health of any puppies we produce.

Labradors are susceptible to a number of inherited conditions and it is vital that anyone breeding Labradors ensures that both parents of any puppies produced have been checked for these conditions before getting a bitch pregnant.

Beside your moral obligation to do so, the consequences of failing in this duty can be serious. Without these clearances, you stand an increased chance of failing to sell your puppies; being sued by angry owners of unhealthy puppies that you have sold to them; having unhealthy puppies returned to you and the cost of their veterinary treatment being laid at your door.

Let's look at these tests in a little more detail.

Eye tests

Progressive retinal atrophy (PRA) is a serious eye disease that causes blindness in Labradors, sometimes at a young age, sometimes later in life. A clear British Veterinary Association (BVA) eye-test certificate means that the dog has been examined by a vet specialising in this field and pronounced free from the disease *at the time of the examination*. It does not mean that the dog does not have the inherited condition, just that he/she displays no sign of it at this time. These basic eye tests should be carried out on breeding animals on an annual basis. If you intend to breed, it is a good idea to get this test done first, then, should your dog fail, you won't have subjected him/her to a general anaesthetic or paid out for the much more expensive hip and elbow tests.

The problem with the eye examination is that it can only tell us the state of the dog's eyes at the time of the test. To get PRA, a dog must have a pair of faulty genes. If only one of the pair is faulty, he/she won't get sick (the healthy gene switches off the faulty one) but can still pass the disease on to the puppies. Fortunately, a DNA test is available: the Optigen test. This shows whether or not the dog you intend to breed from carries the gene for PRA blindness (one faulty gene), is affected by the disease (two faulty genes) or is unaffected (two healthy genes). This is great news for puppy buyers, who now actively look for puppies with Optigen-tested parents.

Hip tests

Hip dysplasia is a potentially crippling disease of the hip joints. The purpose of hip scoring is to help breeders choose parents with good-quality hips. In the UK, the quality of the hips is represented by a numerical score, and the lower it is, the better the hips. A perfect hip has a score of zero, but this is fairly unusual.

The score is expressed by two numbers – one for each hip – written as 5/7 or 5-7 or 5:7. The final hip score is the total of the two figures added together. In this example, the total score is 12. It is also important that the score is fairly balanced, so while 5/7 might be okay, 2/10 – which also gives a score of 12 – is not so good.

If you double the score of the worst hip, you are still looking for something at or under the breed mean score, which in Labradors, at the time of writing, is 12.

In the USA, the score is expressed differently, allocated to one of seven categories. Normal hips are divided into Excellent, Good and Fair, and dysplastic hips are categorised as Mild, Moderate and Severe. There is a borderline category between the two.

What we are looking for in good Labrador breeding stock is a hip score that is significantly better than average. This helps to reduce the chances of the puppies inheriting severe hip problems. It does not *guarantee* that every puppy bred from the dog with a good score will have good hips because, unlike the eye problems discussed above, hip disease is not caused by a single gene, and also, other factors influence the development of your puppy's hips.

Elbow tests

Twenty years ago, few of us had heard of elbow dysplasia. Nowadays, it is increasingly common to come across owners whose dogs and puppies are being treated for this condition. Elbow dysplasia is a broad term given to a number of developmental defects that can occur in the elbow joint of an affected puppy's front leg or legs. These defects mean that the joint doesn't move as freely as it should and the joint becomes prone to osteoarthritis, sometimes at a very young age. Elbow dysplasia causes pain and discomfort in the joint and the dog will eventually become lame as a result. Symptoms may include stiffness that gets worse with exercise, limping, an odd gait, a turned-out foot, or swelling around the joint.

In the UK, a perfect elbow is graded as zero. So ideally, all dogs used for breeding will have an elbow score of 0/0 – one score for each front leg. The worst grade is 3. A puppy's best chance of perfect elbows comes from having two parents with scores of 0/0, and this is what you should be aiming for. The USA grades are similar but no grade is given for a perfect elbow and dysplastic elbows are graded I to III with III being the worst.

Testing for CNM

Centronuclear myopathy, usually referred to as CNM, is a serious disorder affecting Labradors and some other breeds of dog. It's a progressive disease of the muscles, and affected puppies usually start to display symptoms before they are six months old. Affected dogs will have an abnormal gait, and become fatigued easily, and they may have difficulty swallowing because the muscles of the oesophagus are also affected. The prognosis is poor and many dogs with CNM are euthanased.

Just like PRA, this is a recessive disease caused by a faulty gene, and we now have a DNA test for it. If at least one of the parents of a litter is tested clear, none of the puppies will suffer from this devastating condition. CNM is not widespread yet, but it is present in Labradors in the UK and USA, so you might want to ensure that at least one dog from any mating you are involved in has been tested and is clear.

Testing for EIC

Exercise induced collapse (EIC) is another fairly recent discovery, and increasing numbers of responsible breeders are testing for it. EIC is an unpleasant disease that strikes down young and apparently healthy gundogs, often in the prime of their lives, or at the peak of their working or competitive careers.

Dogs that have this disease typically become weak and collapse after a short period (five to twenty minutes) of high-intensity exercise, especially if accompanied by a great deal of excitement. Pet dogs are just as susceptible to the disease as working dogs, but it may go undetected if they do not participate in any intensive activity. Most dogs recover quite quickly from each episode, although a few affected dogs have tragically died. Scientists at the University of Minnesota identified the gene responsible in 2008 and a DNA test is now available.

Having your dog tested

This is not an exhaustive list of tests, and more are being developed. At the time of writing, it is essential that you test for hip, elbow and eye disease before breeding from your Labrador. Up-to-date information is obtainable from the Kennel Club. When deciding on whether or not to test for CNM or EIC, it will be helpful to have some knowledge about the ancestors of the dogs you are considering breeding from, and to consult other more experienced breeders.

In the UK, the British Veterinary Association and the Kennel Club together run the grading schemes for hip and elbow dysplasia. In the USA, testing is done through the Orthopedic Foundation For Animals. The scores are determined by a team of experts who examine X-rays of your dog's hips and elbows. These X-rays are normally carried out under general anaesthetic or heavy sedation, so it makes sense to have them done together. You can arrange this through your local veterinary surgeon. More information about CNM testing can be found on the Animal Health Trust website, and information about EIC testing is available from the University of Minnesota.

These schemes enable breeders to make better breeding choices, and to enable puppy buyers to make better buying decisions. Many of us who write about dogs encourage all puppy buyers to make wise choices when searching for their puppies, and, increasingly, people are avoiding breeders who don't match up.

The DNA tests available to us can be used to give us more rather than less choice, because we can now distinguish carriers from affected dogs. Breeding from carriers is not only safe, if done correctly, but can be beneficial to the health of the breed.

Breeding from carriers and endorsing registrations

It is perfectly acceptable to breed from a carrier of an autosomal recessive disease provided that you mate the carrier dog to a dog that has been tested clear. A carrier has one faulty gene and one healthy one. A clear dog has two healthy genes. Together, they can never pass two faulty genes to a puppy, so none of their puppies will be affected by the disease in question.

However, it is also vital that you tell the new puppy owners what you have done, because some of the puppies will also be carriers, and must only be mated to clear or unaffected dogs. You might want to put an endorsement on the pedigrees of the litter. In the UK, this will help to ensure that they won't be bred from without undergoing the relevant tests. This is not a bad idea with any puppy because it puts the onus on the new owner to carry out health checks before breeding.

What you need to do next

You can see that quite a lot is involved in breeding from your dog. If you think you have what it takes, and are certain you want to breed, the first step is to get those health tests done. You also need to acquire some knowledge and experience in order to choose a suitable mate, and be aware of your role as bitch or stud-dog owner.

The general public is becoming increasingly aware of the risks of inbreeding. When you choose a mate for your dog, bear this in mind. Look at both pedigrees to ensure that the dogs in question are well suited and not too closely related. The Kennel Club offers a service, mateselect, to help you with this.

As the owner of the bitch, your responsibility is to care for your dog during her pregnancy and to act as midwife at the birth. You are also responsible for the health and welfare of the puppies, for worming, weaning and early socialisation. If you want to breed from your bitch, it will help if you attend some births first, and get yourself a mentor – an experienced breeder who is willing to support you, ideally in person, but at least to be available by telephone, at any time of the day and night.

I recommend you buy a copy of the definitive guide for bitch owners, called quite simply, *The Book of the Bitch*, and download a copy of the Kennel Club's guide for breeders. Details of these publications are listed at the back of this book.

As the owner of a stud dog, you are responsible for supervising the mating and ensuring it is successful. You really do need to attend some matings before you take on this important role. Never leave your dog alone to service a bitch – he could be seriously injured. You need to learn how to assist the dog if necessary, how to turn the dog safely during the tie, and how to break the tie in an emergency.

SUMMARY

Breeding from your dog is a really big deal, with risks and few benefits. You may feel this paints a rather negative picture, but the truth is, most people will not benefit from breeding from their pet Labrador, and most pet Labradors will not benefit, either. It is possible that you will enjoy the process, and that you will have the puppy you want at the end of it. It is also possible that it will be an emotionally and financially draining experience that you will never want to repeat.

The hard facts are that unless your dog has distinguished himself, and is health tested to the max, no one will be beating a path to your door for his services as a stud dog. And unless your bitch has passed all the health tests, possesses a superb temperament and distinguished parents, and has been mated to a distinguished stud dog, no one will be beating a path to your door for her puppies.

If this has not put you off, you may well have what it takes! If you decide to go ahead, make sure you have the right dog or bitch, and the time, commitment, resources and support to do the job responsibly. If you can do this, then, with a little luck, you will find the experience both enjoyable and rewarding.

While there is quite a lot of potential for things to go wrong during pregnancy and birth, these are not the only ways in which the pleasures of dog ownership can go awry. In the next chapter, we are going to look at some of the problems that may affect you during the life of your dog, and at how to resolve them.

15

When things go wrong

We've talked quite a bit about problems in this book. I see no point in sweeping them under the carpet. After all, many dogs have problem behaviours and Labradors are no exception. For the most part, though, Labrador problems can be sorted out with a little help, as already discussed.

However, sometimes problems can be more deep-seated and serious. We all have high expectations when we bring a dog into our lives but the truth is that dogs and people are often flawed. There are Labradors out there causing serious difficulties for their families, and families causing serious difficulties for their Labradors, often through no fault of their own.

If you are at the end of your tether with your dog, even if you are contemplating rehoming him or taking him to your local dog rescue, I will not be judging you. This chapter is to offer you the help and advice you need to get your life back on an even keel. It is the chapter I hope you won't need to read. It's about serious problems that you may have at some point in your Labrador's life, either with your dog or that affect your dog. Let's make a start by talking about the challenges of coping with reactive dogs.

Reactive dogs

A well-balanced dog is comfortable in his own skin. He is happy to greet people, and to meet other dogs. That doesn't mean he is never, ever grumpy – dogs are entitled to have likes and dislikes – but it means that, for the most part, he gets along happily in our crazy human world. A reactive dog is not comfortable. He literally overreacts to all kinds of things, either through fear or sometimes through excitement.

If your dog growls when next-door's Poodle won't stop poking him but gets along with other dogs, he is not reactive. He just doesn't like next-door's Poodle.

If he starts bristling and growling whenever another dog approaches him, if walks are becoming a worry because you never know if he is going to growl, or if he tries to hide behind you every time another dog approaches, you have a reactive dog.

Some reactive dogs behave aggressively if they are not allowed to avoid the source of their fear. Others panic, yell or try to escape, but you should assume that a fearful reactive dog may become aggressive if trapped with the source of his fear.

Some reactive dogs are not fearful, but behave in an obsessive or hysterical way. If your dog freezes and trembles with excitement whenever he sees a cat, or barks frantically whenever a vehicle approaches, or attempts to bite at the wheels of passing bicycles, this, too, is a type of reactivity.

Basically, the reactive dog is easily overwhelmed by environmental triggers that do not have the same effect on the majority of well-balanced dogs. Living with a reactive dog can be a very tough and isolating experience. It can affect many aspects of your life and feel as though you are the only person in the world who is having to cope with this.

Fortunately, a lot can be done to help, although, in many cases, the best results are achieved with supervision from a qualified behaviourist. We'll look at how to go about choosing a behaviourist in a moment.

Coping with reactive dogs

Almost certainly, you want your dog to stop being hysterical or angry or whatever emotion he is displaying, but treating reactivity effectively is not to do with changing the way your dog behaves. It is to do with changing the way he feels.

Teaching your dog not to growl at other dogs while he remains fearful or angry about being near to them is simply going to create other unacceptable, possibly more dangerous, behaviours, such as biting or running away. So the objective of the treatment is always to help the dog *feel* calm or happy. We want him to relax so that he can enjoy life and be free from fear and anxiety.

If reactivity has spilled over into serious aggression, you must take immediate steps to prevent him harming anyone – use a muzzle, harness and long line – and seek professional help. But if your dog is simply anxious or excitable in certain situations, it may be worth attempting to improve things yourself. If he is afraid, the first step is to put distance between him and the source of his fear. Give him a break, allow him a chance to relax. If he hates walking past the house with the yappy Chihuahua, walk another way for a while. People often try to force dogs to face their fears, but this is not an effective strategy and it usually just confirms for the dog that there is *everything* to be afraid of. So it is fine to cross the road if a dog your dog hates is approaching. You are not avoiding the issue; you are helping your dog remain calm.

The next step is to help him feel more comfortable at closer proximity to the source of his fear. This means controlling the situation, protecting him from being overwhelmed while at the same time associating the situation he is wary of with something he enjoys. This is called counter-conditioning.

Labradors are often greedy dogs so the use of food is a valuable aid in the counter-conditioning process. Keep your dog far enough away from the source of his excitement or anxiety for him to be able to relax and eat. Use high-value food, such as chunks of roast meat, or slices of sausage. You can ask him to carry out simple tasks in order to win the food, which will help him to concentrate on you. Over time, your objective is to help him feel comfortable close to the source of his reactivity. This is not a process that can be rushed. It may take weeks or months.

Counter-conditioning is not the only way to help a reactive dog. Professional behaviourists have a range of techniques they can offer. They will be able to make a full assessment of your dog, and devise the best approach for his individual problem. Serious aggression is a serious matter. Trying to fix it yourself is not a good idea. If you are simply worried about your mildly reactive dog, or don't feel confident to try some counter-conditioning on your own, it is really important to seek professional help to avoid things getting worse.

Finding a behavourist

The first port of call is your vet. This is not just because the vet may be able to recommend a good local behaviourist, but because for any dog with serious reactivity problems, physical causes should be excluded. The vet will give your dog a thorough examination to make sure he is in good health. Once that is done, you can set about finding a modern behaviourist. The word modern is important in order to find someone who uses the latest scientifically proven techniques to change the way your dog feels about his fears. Some old-school behaviourists, who have not kept up with the latest professional developments, are still around, practising dangerous and outdated methods of behavioural modification. If a behaviourist talks a lot about leadership, encourages you to dominate your dog or tries to teach you ways to show your dog he is at the bottom of the pack, walk away fast. Ideally, in the UK, your behaviourist will be a Certified Clinical Animal Behaviourist (CCAB). This is a qualification awarded by the Association for the Study of Animal Behaviour (ASAB). In the USA, you are looking for a Certified Applied Animal Behaviourist (CAAB) or Associate Applied Animal Behaviourist (ACAAB).

An excellent book that can help you with your reactive dog while you find a professional behaviourist to work with, and afterwards, is *Behaviour Adjustment Training for Fear, Frustration and Aggression in Dogs*. It's by Grisha Stewart, and I recommend you buy a copy (details at the back of this book).

🐾 The serial absconder

Many dogs have a shaky recall. Absconding is different. The absconder runs away and is not interested in coming back, sometimes for hours at a time. This issue is most common in dogs that have been rehomed at some point, and have not forged a good bond with their new family, or in dogs that have powerful hunting instincts and have been allowed to develop a habit of chasing wildlife.

Absconding can almost always be cured, but it can take a very long time to turn an absconder around, especially one with a chasing habit. It requires a lot of determination on the part of the owner to keep going with the process. As a rough guide, it may take you as long as your dog has been absconding to achieve an effective cure. So if he has been running away for a year or more, expect to spend a year or more on a cure. Creating a deep-rooted association between recall and great rewards is a key factor in overcoming absconding, but equally important is the permanent prevention of running away, and the establishment of a history or pattern of successful recall.

The absconding dog must wear a harness attached to a long line whenever he is outdoors for the duration of the initial training process. This will probably mean for months. So get your dog a harness that fits well, and a long line that is tough, washable and resists tangling or kinking.

The principle of long-line training is that the dog wears the line at all times. You can't have him wear it on some occasions and not on others – he will almost certainly figure out when you have control of him and when you do not, and behave accordingly. The line and harness have to become a part of his life for as long as it takes him to forget his difficult past. You might find my book *Total Recall* helpful in retraining your absconder.

🐾 Families in crisis

Both absconding and reactivity are problems that require a huge amount of input from the dog's main carer. If that person has the time and resources to give to the task, a good outcome is likely. But sometimes, if these problems arise when the person in question is barraged with other difficulties, the challenge may be too great, and the relationship between dog and family can go spiralling downhill.

The last thing that occurs to most of us when we arrive home with a new puppy in our arms, is that we might one day have to give him up. The hard truth is that thousands of dogs are given up by their owners every year, for many different reasons. Labrador rescue societies have a steady stream of dogs through their doors.

Sometimes dogs are given up because people's circumstances have drastically changed. Owners may have to work longer hours or their work may take them abroad. People die, get divorced, lose their jobs, become sick or disabled. Dogs, like children, may suffer in these circumstances.

We are all aware of the mantra 'a dog is for life'. People often tell me that they would never, under any circumstance, part with their dog. But life can be complicated, and for some people, no matter how responsible or caring they are, priorities change, and sometimes what was once a great environment for a dog is no longer an appropriate home.

Doing the right thing

There are good reasons why you should try to keep your dog and deal with his problems within the family environment – *if you can reasonably do so*. This is where he feels safe, and if you have had him from a puppy, there will be a strong bond between you. Problem dogs are often passed on more than once, so if you have the resources to help your dog yourself, perhaps with some professional help, then that is probably his best chance of a good outcome.

However, keeping your dog and struggling against all odds to do so, is not necessarily in his best interests. If your physical or mental health is not great at the moment, and being worsened by problems with your dog, you may be better to put yourself first. If you are caring for a sick child or a dying relative, your family's needs may outweigh those of your dog, and indeed, if he has behavioural problems, you may simply lack the resources to be able to help him adequately at this point in your life.

I cannot tell you whether or not you should keep your dog. These are desperate decisions and everyone's situation is unique. I can only tell you that if you do decide to part with him, there is a right way to go about it, and several very wrong ways that you should endeavour to avoid.

Rehoming

Unless you are very experienced and knowledgeable about screening potential new owners, private rehoming is a risky business. Unscrupulous people may take 'free to a good home' dogs and use them for unsavoury purposes – indiscriminate breeding or even dog fighting. As a private individual, it would be difficult for you to check the credentials of any new owner, or to assess their suitability. It may be tempting to give your dog to a friend, but remember that if your dog has a problem, you are effectively giving your friend a problem, too, and he/she may not be sufficiently motivated or knowledgeable to cope.

Rehoming is really a job at which dog-rescue centres excel, and the best chance of a good and permanent home for your dog lies with one of these dedicated organisations. They are able to assess dogs with behavioural problems and match them with owners who can cope. They will go into the homes of prospective new owners and ensure that they are genuine, loving people, who will treasure your dog. You simply cannot replicate this kind of process by yourself.

The rehoming process

People who have to part with a dog usually feel very judged and embarrassed by the whole situation. They are often afraid to approach a rescue centre and risk being labelled 'that awful person who couldn't cope with his/her dog'. On the contrary, a good rescue centre will not judge you at all. The staff there would far rather you gave up your dog under their guidance, as part of a carefully controlled process, than failed to provide for his needs, or attempted to rehome him by yourself. They will also be able to offer you support and advice as you make your decision, so it is worth approaching them early on in the process, even before you have made up your mind.

If you need to rehome your dog because you cannot cope with his behaviour, you must be brutally honest about his faults. This enables rescue-centre staff to match the dog with the right owners, people who are capable of dealing with any problems he may have. This in turn helps to prevent your dog being passed from home to home. A new owner will discover his faults soon enough, and many experienced dog owners are willing to take on a dog with some problems, provided they understand what they are getting into.

Before you decide

If you are struggling with your dog's training, and are thinking of rehoming him for that reason, do consider very carefully whether you could still learn how to train him yourself, perhaps with a temporary break to address any other problems. Asking a friend to look after your dog for a few days is often a good idea if you have reached crisis point. It gives you a chance to think about what you are doing and the best way forwards. Consulting a behaviourist isn't cheap, but you may feel the weight lift from your shoulders once you have some professional help and guidance and a plan to work with.

Sometimes people struggle on with routines that cause them stress because they are too wrapped up in their problem to step back and see a simpler way out. It can be a great relief, for example, for the owner of an absconder finally to accept that the dog needs to be on a training lead at all times for the next few months. There is no shame in this and it is a stage in the learning process. Young dogs can be unbelievably destructive and many owners are astonished at how the considered use of a crate at night can restore harmony to the home.

It is not unusual for inexperienced dog owners to be in constant conflict with their dog because they don't understand how to motivate him. Abandoning old-fashioned training methods and switching to positive-reinforcement training using food rewards has been the saving of many a dog and his owner.

If you have truly come to the end of the road, don't be ashamed, but do turn to your local Labrador rescue for help and advice. They will help you secure a safe and happy future for your dog.

Most problem Labradors do stay with their families, though, and in most cases, their problems can be managed well enough to allow families to enjoy their dog once more. In many cases, with the right help, problems such as absconding and reactivity can be completely overcome. After the hard work you put into your dog, it is very rewarding to realise that you no longer have to worry about him and he is, in fact, a normal Labrador once more. As the years go by, you may even forget that he ever was a problem dog.

One of the tough things about loving and living with dogs, is that their lives compared with ours are relatively short. It sometimes seems that no sooner have we left puddles and puppy toys behind than we see a hint of the senior years to come. We notice a certain stiffness as he stretches on wakening in the morning, and a subtle greying of his muzzle as it is pressed into our hand in greeting.

Caring for an older dog can pose a few concerns but it can also be a great pleasure. Making the most of your older dog, and giving him the support he needs, is the subject of the next chapter.

16

Your senior dog

Getting old is a fact of life, and, on the whole, dogs cope with it very well. Free as they are from concerns about who will take care of them, or what will happen to those they love after they've gone, dogs are in blissful ignorance of the possibilities that lie ahead. It is we humans who do the worrying, make decisions on their behalf and ensure that they are well cared for and comfortable in their old age.

Senior Labradors still have a lot to give.

Most Labradors remain active and reasonably fit almost to the end of their days, but just like people, they can become less mobile, a bit stiff and creaky, and less resistant to illness as they enter their twilight years. Fortunately, there is much you can do to keep your senior dog in good health, and we'll be looking at common ailments of old age, and what you can do to support your dog during this phase of his life.

Probably the single most important thing you can ever do for your ageing dog is keep him slim, which brings us to the question of how best to feed and exercise your elderly friend.

Feeding the senior dog

How you feed your older Labrador will depend to some extent on him. Some dogs lose their voracious appetite as they age and become increasingly picky and disinterested in food. One important thing to be aware of is that age-related changes in appetite tend to be a gradual thing. If your dog *suddenly* goes off his food, it may be a warning sign that he is not well, so do take him along to your vet for a check-up.

Many Labradors will carry on consuming as much food as ever and may start to put on a little weight. This is something you should try to avoid. As your dog ages, his metabolism may slow down a little, and, especially if he is losing mobility, he may be taking less exercise than before. This means that he won't be needing quite as many calories. One way to deal with this is to reduce the quantity of his food. Some senior-branded foods have lower calorie levels, which allows you to carry on filling your dog's bowl to the same level as before.

Some commercial foods include additives that, the claim is, improve joint health – usually glucosamine and chondroitin. These supplements do seem to have an effect on joint tissues that have been isolated in a laboratory, but it is less clear whether or not taking them orally allows glucosamine or chondroitin to reach the joints in sufficient quantities to have a beneficial effect. Trials on humans have been disappointing, although a small study on dogs in 2007 concluded that glucosamine and chondroitin did have a positive clinical effect on dogs with osteoarthritis.

It's up to you how you feed your older dog. If he is still eating well, remaining slim and taking plenty of exercise, he'll probably be just fine on the food he has been eating for the last few years. If he seems to be getting a little portly, you can simply reduce the quantity of food a little. If he gobbles up the food really quickly and is disappointed with your rations, you can put his meals into a slow feed bowl to keep him happy. If you want to give your dog glucosamine supplements, these can be purchased separately. Your vet will be able to advise you of the current state of research into supplements and help you decide if these are worthwhile for your dog.

Caring for old bones

A significant proportion of elderly Labradors suffer from some degree of arthritis or joint damage as they age. One of the best ways you can help and support a dog with joint problems is to keep his weight down through portion control, but there are other important factors to consider. Maintaining an appropriate schedule of regular exercise is a key one, as is pain relief and generally keeping your dog comfortable.

Many old dogs still enjoy a daily walk but may not be able to walk as far or for as long as they used to when young. If you find your dog reluctant to go with you, it may be that he would appreciate shorter and more frequent walks now, rather than a daily long hike; or it may be that he is in need of pain medication. Some dog owners have a certain amount of reluctance to put their dogs on daily

Older dogs may need more attention and special care.

pain medication. They don't like the idea of giving their dog chemicals, and have heard that painkillers can have serious side effects. This is something you really do need to discuss with a trusted vet. Many dogs do not suffer from adverse side effects and their daily quality of life may be dramatically improved by pain relief.

It is worth considering, too, that dogs cannot tell us when they are in pain, and most dogs hide pain very well. Often, we only realise how much they were suffering when the pain is lifted. Constant pain is very debilitating and so it is important not to dismiss this form of medication out of hand.

As our dogs get older, they often need more padding in their beds in order to get comfortable. You might want to consider raising your dog's bed off the floor a few centimetres, to keep him out of draughts, and providing him with a thicker mattress. If he is allowed on your bed or on the sofa, he may need a step to help him get up there. If your car is quite high, you may need to make or buy him a ramp to help him get in and out. These little considerations can make life a lot more pleasant for an ageing dog.

Lumps and bumps

As your dog ages, it is a good idea to check him over regularly for unusual lumps and bumps. Run your hands along his flanks and belly, neck and shoulders and down each leg, and feel gently inside his groins and armpits. If you find an unusual lump, don't panic. Harmless fatty lumps are extremely common in elderly dogs. However, it is important to get new lumps and bumps checked by your vet, so make an appointment for sometime in the next week or so, and show your vet the lump you found. He may want to take a small biopsy to check that all is well. The reason for paying attention to lumps and bumps is that, just like people, Labradors become more susceptible to cancer as they age, and early treatment improves the chances of a good outcome for the dog. You'll probably find any obvious lumps while stroking and petting your dog, but a thorough, deliberate check at regular intervals is always a good idea.

A 1999 study of longevity in over three thousand dogs found that 16 per cent of deaths were attributable to cancer, and lumps and bumps are not necessarily the first sign something is wrong. A common type of cancer in dogs is lymphoma, which usually presents initially as swollen glands, followed by more general symptoms, such as weight loss, loss of appetite and digestive upsets. Some cancers may respond well to treatment, if started early enough. So it is worth being aware of subtle changes in your dog. If he seems off colour to you, even if you can't quite put your finger on why, drop into your vet's office and have him checked over.

Hearing, eyesight and continence

You may have been putting your dog's poor recall down to deafness for quite a while now, but there comes a point in many Labrador's lives when hearing and eyesight may genuinely begin to fail. There isn't a great deal we can do to reverse hearing loss, other than buy a louder whistle, which may help for a while, but we can teach our dogs to recognise and obey hand signals. It is also possible to buy a collar that vibrates and teach your dog to recall to that. Dogs that are going deaf may sometimes bark more, and be alarmed when people make them jump. Some consideration is necessary in the way you, and other people, approach your dog, especially if he loses his hearing completely.

Failing eyesight can sometimes be treated, depending on the cause. Labradors are susceptible to a form of inherited blindness that is common in many pedigree breeds of dog. This can affect dogs at quite a young age, but is more usual in older dogs. Loss of vision due to cataracts may be treatable by surgery. In either case, if you think your dog is losing his sight, it is important to have him looked at by a vet. If loss of vision is permanent, you'll need to be careful with your dog. Make

Senses can diminish as your Labrador ages.

sure that stairs and steep steps are gated, and don't rearrange the furniture. A blind or partially sighted dog can live a happy and fulfilling life, and still enjoy his walks and outings. You just need to supervise him a little more closely.

Elderly dogs sometimes lose control of their bowels or bladder or both. Don't assume that this is the end of the road for your dog. It may be treatable. The best thing to do is to ask the vet to check him over and let you know whether the incontinence is fixable, or whether it is going to be a permanent problem for you and your dog.

Heart problems and other ailments of old age

Around 8 per cent of dogs succumb to heart disease according to the 1999 study of three thousand dogs mentioned above. According to Vet Compass (an organisation that shares and analyses veterinary clinical information), it is the fifth most common cause of death, and signs of heart problems are something to look out for in your elderly dog. Other organs can fail, too – kidneys, for example, can cause problems.

If your old friend has a persistent cough, or doesn't seem able to walk as far as he used to, it's time for a check-up at the vet's. If he is thirstier than normal or weeing more than normal, get him looked at. In fact, any change of habit in an elderly dog should be investigated. Don't just put it down to old age. Crying at night, unusual barking, not wanting to go out, not settling at night, not eating properly – these are all signs that something isn't right. Your vet is the best person to figure out what that something might be. It's always worth a check-up. Don't forget, many problems of old age can be treated and give the dog months or even years more of active life.

When to let go

As the end of your pet's life draws near, there may come a time when you will be called upon to make the hardest decision. Many of us hope that our very old dog will just go quietly in his sleep, but sadly, the end of life is not usually that simple. The option for euthanasia is not available to humans in the UK, but it is available for our dogs. Choosing when to use that option is an intensely personal and tough decision. When people are dying, we accept that all we can do is make them comfortable. Palliative care is an important branch of medicine that many of us will depend upon in our twilight months. Palliative care for dogs is a somewhat newer concept.

What follows is a personal story to illustrate my own slant on a difficult subject. It's about an end-of-life decision I was involved in as a teenager. When I was young, if a dog was diagnosed with terminal cancer, as my Golden Retriever, Rob, was, the dog was normally put to sleep on the spot, or very shortly afterwards. Our vet made the diagnosis in his surgery and we took our dog home so we could have a last couple of days together. The vet then came out to put him to sleep in his own home. At this point, medication was controlling his discomfort absolutely and he was in full control of his bodily functions. Still continent, and able-bodied. Still enjoying life. That would not be the case, our vet assured us, for much longer.

There was not much in the way of cancer treatment for dogs then. No one suggested that we extend his life with drugs. He might have lived a little longer, but it was not considered to be an option by my family or our vet. He never suffered, apart from the mild symptoms that had led us to the vet in the first place, and he spent his last couple of days pottering about the house and garden quite happily. My experience as a teenager reflects a different approach to the end-of-life care chosen by some families for their dogs in modern times. I have no regrets about the decision we made. It was the first time, at just eighteen years old, that I had been involved in such a decision, and I have had to make similar decisions in the intervening years.

Nowadays, there is perhaps a tendency to drag out a dog's life to the bitter end, even when quality of life is really all but gone. It is common practice now for dog owners to wait until the dog is showing signs of suffering before putting him to sleep. This is understandable. No one wants to put a dog to sleep, and in some cases, I think owners feel they will be judged and attract disapproval if they end their dog's life too early. Timing is a very difficult thing to get right. My personal view is that waiting for the suffering to *start* before making that final decision may not always be of benefit to our beloved dogs. Of course, with younger dogs, especially if the illness is not terminal, a whole range of other factors have to be considered. The dog's quality of life during convalescence has to be balanced against the potential for quality of life in the future. But with elderly dogs, once serious illness has set in, there is very often only one way to go, and that is downhill.

Our family dog, and my childhood friend all those years ago, could probably have had a few more days of joyful living, possibly a few more weeks, and we may have deprived him of that time. The risk that he would then have begun to suffer, perhaps terribly, even for a short time, was not acceptable to us. Knowing that he never suffered at all was, and still is, a comfort to me.

I am telling this story to illustrate that waiting until the bitter end is not the only option, and to show that it is possible to end a dog's life, knowing that it is the right thing to do, even though he seems well at that moment in time, without suffering from regret afterwards. I am also one of those who feel that dignity is important to dogs. I have no evidence for this. It's just a personal view. I was

Old dogs still enjoy a nice relaxed day out.

saddened to read, a while ago, about a person who had nursed her elderly dog through weeks of incontinence before death. She talked about 'peri-care' and 'diapers' and the difficulties of caring for ageing and incontinent dogs. I was sad for her and for her dog. For me, that would not be an option. I feel that dignity, in some sense of the word, does matter to dogs, and that an elderly dog would be very distressed by being unable to keep itself clean. Knowing that there is no hope of recovery, and believing that a dog has no concept of, or fear of, death, is enough to keep me from going down that route. This is, of course, an intensely personal topic, and everyone will feel differently about dignity and a dog's ability to look after his own hygiene.

In any case, there is no doubt that looking after a very ill dog can be tough, what with mess and stress, the smell of sickness and disinfectant, and the drain of broken nights. It is natural to be torn two ways – to want it to end, but to want to spend a little more time with the dog. I think sometimes people are afraid that making the decision to end their dog's life might be based on their own convenience. So they make the wrong decision, *for all the right reasons*. They are trying to put the dog first, and to ignore their own needs. So they keep the dog alive for a few more weeks when, in some cases, ending the dog's life at an earlier stage might have been a kinder decision.

Perhaps we are a little too reluctant to make use of this option, which is readily available for our dogs and can prevent a great deal of suffering. My story about Rob has been posted on the Labrador site for several years and is one of the more discussed and commented articles on the website. The comments show how much people care about this subject and how desperately people want to get this right for their dogs. 'Better a week too early than a day too late' is not my quote, but it sums up how I feel about this sad topic.

You cannot predict the future. You cannot know exactly when your dog will start hurting or how much. You have to make a decision based on your individual dog and this is often best done in conjunction with your vet. The vet will be able to tell you what the outlook is for your Labrador and help you keep him pain free and happy for as long as possible. When the time comes to make that final decision, try not to torment yourself, wondering if he might have lasted a few days more. If there is no hope left, and the only way is down, having the courage to let your dog slip peacefully away may be the last truly noble gesture you can offer him, and a just reward for all his years of devotion.

Every Labrador we embrace within our families will carve his own special place in our hearts. At the end of his journey, we will mourn the passing of our old companion, but we need have no regrets. A dog lives life right here, in the moment, and you can be sure that your friend took care to enjoy every single day of his. The pain of parting does grow less with time. One day, you may be ready to bring another young Labrador into your life, and start this amazing journey once more. In the meantime, it's important to focus on the happy times and on the good memories that you will surely hold in your heart.

In the next and final chapter of this book, we are going to look at having fun with your dog and creating some nice memories for you to treasure. There are some games that you can play with Labradors of any age, which your old friend will almost certainly enjoy. These games are great for a rainy day, for dogs that are on a restricted-exercise regime, or for senior Labradors that are simply too old to want to go for a five-mile hike before breakfast each day.

These senior years really can be golden years. I hope you enjoy them, and do try not to worry about what the future will bring for your elderly dog. With the loving care and attention that you give him every day, and a few concessions to his age, your old friend's retirement should be long, happy and fulfilled.

Love and loyalty never fades.

17

Fun games for Labradors of any age

We have travelled along through our Labrador story, from puppyhood to old age. We've conquered biting, sleepless nights and puddles, weathered the storms of adolescence and come out safely on the other side. We have looked at the ups and downs of life with the world's most amazing dog, journeyed through years of faithful friendship together, and seen our dear companion safely through to old age and beyond.

We can't end there of course! Life with a Labrador is all about having fun, so let's conclude this story by doing what Labradors do best, and immerse ourselves in some enjoyable games. Each one of the four described here can be played with Labradors of any age.

Make the most of your Labrador's enthusiasm for life.

Find the toy

Choose a toy your dog really loves and is happy to carry around. Use the name of the toy a lot while your dog is holding and playing with it. Now sit your dog, or get someone to hold him, and let him see you take the toy through an open doorway and place it on the floor in full view in another room.

Go back to your dog and tell him to find his rope/ball/teddy in a happy, upbeat voice. Tell him how clever he is when he finds it. Pet him, fuss him and give him a treat. Repeat several times. Now it is time to make things more complicated.

Making it more difficult

This time place the toy out of his view, where he cannot easily see it until he is *in the room*. Don't hide it under anything yet. You need to build up his skill gradually. Repeat several times. Then make the toy a little more difficult to find than before.

After a few more repetitions, you can start to make the game even more challenging by hiding the toy under a cardboard box or a cushion. The secret is to add the level of difficulty very slowly, so that the dog does not get disheartened.

Bloodhound!

Tracking games are great fun for any dog, but Labradors love them. Try laying a scent trail for your dog, with a treat at the end, and watch him follow it with his nose. You can do this outdoors or on a washable floor, and you'll need a few simple items of equipment.

A scent marker, to lay your trail, can be a piece of cloth rubbed in some crushed sausage, or some other yummy, smelly treat. You will need some more of the same for the treat at the end of the trail. Lay your first trails in a straight line on an open piece of ground, and make them very short. Keep your dog out of sight while you prepare. Mark the start of the trail with a cone or a rock, so that you know where to begin tracking. Drag your cloth along for about a metre and place the treat at the end.

Now fetch your dog and take him to your start marker. Watch him sniff around and follow the scent to the treat. Gradually, you can start to make the game more fun, laying longer trails, and making them wiggly rather than straight. After a few weeks of practising, you will be able to lay quite complicated trails for your dog to play the tracking game.

Four paws in a box

Every dog owner should have a go at this one. It may seem like a trivial party trick but it is a great learning tool and will help you create a brand-new behaviour through shaping (see page 102). The sheer potential of the clicker will really become apparent, and your skill with it will expand rapidly as you work through the game. Not only is shaping fun, dogs that are regularly engaged in shaping sessions become extremely innovative, offering lots of new behaviours in order to find the one that earns them a reward.

Preparation

At the start of the shaping process, you establish a baseline behaviour for your dog. In this case, that can be interacting with the box in a simple way, such as touching it with his nose, or with a paw. All the equipment you need is a shallow cardboard box, some treats and a clicker. The sides of the box need be no more than ten centimetres (three or four inches) high. Just cut down a bigger box if you don't have a shallow one. He should be able to stand with all four feet inside it without being uncomfortable. As with all new games, you need a quiet, distraction-free place to begin. A carpeted floor is ideal so that the box doesn't slip around if he gets excited and takes a flying leap into it.

Practical steps

The first step is to get the dog interested in the box. Any kind of interest will do. Some dogs are just plain nosy. You can guarantee that anything you place on the floor will be thoroughly examined and checked over for goodies. My spaniels are like this. Place a box on the floor and you can be sure they'll rush over to see what's inside. With this kind of dog, you're halfway there before you have even started.

Some Labradors are just not in that place. 'There's a box on the floor?' Yawn. 'Whatever,' is the kind of reaction you get. This dog is going to need an incentive even to look at the box, never mind get in it. So you'll need to be ready to lure a little. Here are some steps you can work through.

Step one – attention on the box

Place the box on the carpet. Mark (with a clicker or a word, 'Yes,' for instance) and reward (with a treat) any attention that the dog gives to the box. This attention can include staring at the box, moving towards the box and touching the box with any part of his body.

Follow each mark with a reward – throw or place the reward well away from the box. When the dog is repeatedly returning to give the box some attention, move on to the next step.

Step two – touching the box

Now be more demanding. Stop marking the dog for looking at and approaching the box. Mark him only for touching it with any part of his body. When he is repeatedly touching the box, move on.

Step two (a) – what if he ignores the box?

You can get him interested in approaching it by placing treats inside. This is a lure, so you will want to get rid of it quite quickly.

Place a treat (lure) in the box. Mark the dog as soon as he touches the box, throw his treat (reward) away from the box, and repeat twice more. Then wait for the dog to approach the box of his own free will. Keep waiting – and waiting! Count in your head to a hundred. If the dog is still ignoring the box, lure him to it again.

Within a short space of time, the dog will be touching the box with his nose, or with a paw, *without the lure.*

Step three – one paw in the box

Look for the dog actually placing a paw inside the box. This usually happens quite quickly, so be ready for it. As soon as you see his paw touch the bottom of the box, mark and reward. Place the treat away from the box so that he has to take his paw out to get it. Be ready to mark and reward as soon as he returns for another go.

Step four – four paws in the box

From one paw, you can proceed to two paws in the box, then look for a third and, finally, a fourth. Back paws can be harder than front paws, so you may need to mark and reward one or two back paws separately for a while, before trying for all four paws at once.

Keep your sessions short. Set aside a set number of treats at the beginning of each session and stop when they are all gone. Don't keep going until the dog gets bored or is full. Twenty treats are fine for a session for most dogs. When you have mastered this trick, you can use a slightly smaller box, then a much smaller one, until your dog will put all four paws in a tiny box and balance there for his treat.

Learning to stand in a box isn't a vital life skill, so it doesn't matter if you win or lose. It is, however, a fun way to learn some very useful training skills and to get lots of attention and focus from your dog.

Freeze!

This is another game with useful applications. Have your dog move around near to you. Keep throwing him tiny treats to hold his attention and, if necessary, dance around to keep him moving and watching you.

Now suddenly stop and freeze. As soon as he copies you and stops moving, mark (with a word or a click from your clicker) and reward him by throwing a treat behind him and away from you. Now start dancing around again. Each time you freeze, wait for him to freeze, too, and immediately mark and reward.

Now you can start to add a cue word. Dance around, say 'Freeze' and stop dancing. Mark and reward the dog when he stops.

Making it more difficult

Now start throwing the treats farther away and saying 'Freeze' when he has picked up the treat and is starting to return. To begin with, he may carry on running towards you before he freezes, but as long as you always throw the treat well behind him, he will soon start to freeze farther away from you.

Freeze is not just a fun game, it can also be a useful cue to give a dog that is heading towards danger or getting too far away. It is easily developed into the stop whistle that you'll need if you ever decide to have a go at gundog training.

Other games

There are many more games you can play with your Labrador, and also puzzle toys you can buy. The Nina Ottoson range is very good. Nowadays, the boundaries between games and training are very blurred. In fact, with modern methods, training is such fun for dogs that to them it is just one huge game.

With all these games, and any kind of training, it pays to make haste slowly, and stop while the dog is having fun. If you want your dog to enjoy it more and carry on for longer, use better rewards. Most dogs will enjoy playing 'find the toy' three times in a row for a pat and a kind word, but if they are playing for chunks of chicken, they will keep going a good deal longer. Stop each game after five or ten minutes, and your dog will be keen to play again next time.

Life with a Labrador

Now, I think, we really have come to the end of our journey. My passion is helping people enjoy their dogs. So if these pages have helped at all as you struggle with teething and heelwork, or put your mind at rest as you journey through the big and bouncy juvenile years, I am glad. My aim was to make your path a smoother one, to take away some of the worry and stress involved in caring for your first Labrador, and to help you and your dog relax and enjoy one another.

Of course, troubles will come and go, and no book can ever replace the help of real live human beings. Only so much detail can be included in a book that covers every aspect of a Labrador's life and care. Having a good relationship with your vet is important, and if you are having problems with your dog that aren't addressed here, or you simply need to talk about your Labrador or be comforted by others who love Labradors, too, do join the Labrador forum. It is a wonderful, supportive, online community of people who love Labradors.

If you want some more in-depth information on the first four months of your new puppy's life, you might enjoy *The Happy Puppy Handbook*, and if you like the idea of teaching your dog a single important skill by following a detailed training programme, you might enjoy my first book, *Total Recall*.

Enjoy your dog

Before we part company, I just want to remind you to spend as much time as you can with your lovely friend. There is no better dog to share your life with than a Labrador Retriever and the years pass by all too quickly.

Modern families are often very busy, and it is easy to overlook the ones we love, especially the four-legged ones. When I was a child, dogs had more freedom and more company. Homes were usually occupied during the day, and dogs and children were free to play in the streets together and return home whenever they wanted. Nowadays, people are often juggling the needs of their dogs and kids with several hours of work. Traffic volume is on another scale, and dogs cannot safely roam the streets. Indeed, many dogs spend a substantial part of their lives entirely alone.

Labradors have weathered these changes and adapted to the modern world with stoic good humour, but they are essentially a very social dog and bask in the warmth of human company. If you can spare a little time each day to train your dog, so that he is welcome to go with you when you visit friends or pop down to your local pub, you and your dog will be able to spend more time together, and this will mean a great deal to him.

If I had to sum up the essence of the Labrador with a single word, it would be 'enthusiasm'. There is nothing a Labrador doesn't want to be involved with, or to be a part of. In his world, there is no walk too short, no meal too small, no gesture of friendship too fleeting to be disregarded. All of life's experiences, great and small, are prized and savoured equally. His love of living is complete, and best of all, he'd love nothing more than to share it all with you.

✿ Resources

Useful books

1. **Evans, J.M. and White, Kay,** *The Book of the Bitch* (Ringpress Books, 2002)
2. **Mattinson, Pippa,** *Total Recall* – a complete and force free recall training programme for puppies and adult dogs (Quiller, 2012)
3. **Mattinson, Pippa,** *The Happy Puppy Handbook* – a definitive guide to puppy care and early training (Ebury, 2014)
4. **Pryor, Karen,** *Clicker Training for Dogs* (Ringpress Books, 2002)
5. **Stewart, Grisha,** *Behaviour Adjustment Training for Fear, Frustration and Aggression in Dogs* (Dogwise Publishing, 2012)

Useful websites

1. **The Labrador Site**
   www.thelabradorsite.com
2. **The Labrador Forum**
   www.thelabradorforum.com
3. **The Kennel Club (UK)**
   www.thekennelclub.org.uk
4. **The United Kennel Club (USA)**
   www.ukcdogs.com
5. **The American Kennel Club (USA)**
   www.akc.org
6. **The Labrador Retriever Club of Great Britain**
   www.thelabradorretrieverclub.com
7. **The Labrador Retriever Club of America**
   www.thelabradorclub.com
8. **British Veterinary Association**
   www.bva.co.uk
9. **American Veterinary Association**
   www.avma.org
10. **World Small Animal Veterinary Association**
    www.wsava.org
11. **Orthopedic Foundation For Animals**
    www.offa.org

Training and trainers

1. **The Gundog Club**
   www.thegundogclub.co.uk
2. **North American Hunting Retriever Association (NAHRA)**
   www.nahra.org
3. **Totally Dog Training**
   www.totallydogtraining.com
4. **Association of Pet Dog Trainers (APDT UK)**
   www.apdt.co.uk
5. **Victoria Stillwell Positive Dog Trainers (VSPDT – USA)**
   www.positively.com
6. **Karen Pryor Academy Dog Trainers (KPA CPT – USA)**
   www.karenpryoracademy.com

Sports and activities

1. **Canicross Trailrunners**
   www.canicross.org.uk
2. **Agility UK**
   www.baa.uk.net
3. **Agility USA**
   www.usdaa.com
4. **British Flyball Association**
   www.flyball.org.uk
5. **North American Flyball Association**
   www.flyball.org
6. **North America Diving Dogs**
   www.northamericadivingdogs.com

Behaviourists

1. **Association of Pet Behaviour Councellors**
   www.apbc.org.uk
2. **Coape Association of Pet Behaviourists & Trainers**
   www.capbt.org
3. **Certified Animal Behaviourists (CAAB – USA)**
   www.animalbehaviorsociety.org

Holidays and outings

1. **Government information**
   www.gov.uk/take-pet-abroad/overview
2. **Dog Friendly Britain**
   www.dogfriendlybritain.co.uk
3. **Bring Fido**
   www.bringfido.com
4. **Pets Welcome**
   www.petswelcome.com

Labrador Rescue Organisations UK

1. **Black Retriever X Rescue**
   www.blackretrieverx.co.uk
2. **Labrador Retriever Rescue North West**
   www.homealabrador.net
3. **Labrador Retriever Rescue Southern England**
   www.labrador-rescue.org.uk
4. **Labrador Rescue South East and Central**
   www.loveyourlabrador.co.uk
5. **The Labrador Rescue Trust**
   www.labrador-rescue.com
6. **The Labrador Lifeline Trust**
   www.labrador-lifeline.co.uk
7. **Labrador Rescue Kent**
   www.labrescuekent.co.uk
8. **Labrador Retriever Rescue Scotland**
   www.lrrss.co.uk
9. **Labrador Welfare (North East)**
   www.labradorwelfare.org

Labrador Rescue Organisations USA are listed on The Labrador Site
www.thelabradorsite.com/rescue-societies/

References

1. **Arhant, C., Bubna-Littitz, H., Bartels, A., Futschik, A., Troxler, J.,** 'Behaviour of smaller and larger dogs: Effects of training methods, inconsistency of owner behaviour, and level of engagement in activities with the dog' *Applied Animal Behaviour Science* (2010)
2. **Blackwell, E.J., Twells, C., Seawright, A., Casey, R.A.,** 'The relationship between training methods and the occurrence of behaviour problems, as reported by owners, in a population of domestic dogs.' *Journal of Veterinary Behavior* (2008)
3. **Bradshaw, J., Blackwell, E., Casey, R.,** 'Dominance in domestic dogs: useful construct or bad habit?' *Journal of Veterinary Behavior* (2009)
4. **Egenvall, A., Hagman, R., Bonnett, B.N., Hedhammar, A., Olson, P., Lagerstedt, A.S.,** 'Breed risk of pyometra in insured dogs in Sweden' *Journal of Veterinary Internal Medicine* (2001)
5. **Feuerbacher, E., Wynne, C.D.,** 'Most domestic dogs (*Canis lupus familiaris*) prefer food to petting: population, context, and schedule effects in concurrent choice' *Journal of the Experimental Analysis of Behavior* (2014)
6. **Fukuzawa, M., Hayashi, N.,** 'Comparison of three different reinforcements of learning in dogs' *Journal of Veterinary Behavior* (2013)
7. **Glickman, L.T., Glickman, N.W., Schellenberg, D.B., Raghaven, M., Lee, T.,** 'Non dietary risk factors for gastric dilation and volvulus in large and giant

breed dogs' *Journal of the American Veterinary Medical Association* (2000)

8. **Glickman, L.T., Glickman, N.W., Schellenberg, D.B., Simpson, K., Lantz, G.C.,** 'Multiple risk factors for gastric dilation-volvulus syndrome in dogs: a practioner/owner case-control study' *Journal of the American Animal Hospital Association* (1997)

9. **Glickman, L.T., Glickman, N.W., Perez, C. M., Schellenberg, D.B., Lantz, G.C.,** 'Analysis of risk factors for gastric dilation and dilation-volvulus in dogs' *Journal of the American Veterinary Medical Association* (1994)

10. **Hart, B.L.,** 'Effect of gonadectomy on subsequent development of age related cognitive impairment in dogs' *Journal of the American Veterinary Medical Association* (2001)

11. **Hart, B.L., Hart, L.A., Thigpen, A.P., Willits, N.H.,** 'Long term health effects of neutering dogs: comparison of Labrador Retrievers with Golden Retrievers' *PLOS one* (2014)

12. **Herron, M.E., Shofer, F.S., Reisner, I.,** 'Survey of the use and outcome of confrontational and non-confrontational training methods in client-owned dogs showing undesirable behaviours' *Applied Animal Behaviour Science* (2009)

13. **Hilby, E.F., Rooney, N.J., Bradshaw, J.W.S.,** 'Dog training methods, their use, effectiveness and interaction with behaviour and welfare' *Animal Behaviour* (2004)

14. **Lewis, T., Blott, S. and Wooliams, J.,** 'Genetic Evaluation of Hip Score in *Labrador Retrievers*' *PLOS one* (2010)

15. **Rooney, N., Cowan, S.,** 'Training methods and owner dog interactions. Links with dog behaviour and learning ability' *Applied Animal Behaviour Science* (2011)

16. **Torres De La Riva, G., Hart, B.L., Farver, T.B., Oberbauer, A.M., Messam, L.L., Willits, N., Hart, L.A.,** 'Neutering dogs: effect on joint disorders and cancers in *Golden Retrievers*' *PLOS one* (2013)

17. **Zink, M.C., Farhoody, P., Elser, S.E., Ruffini, L.D., Gibbons, T.A., Rieger, R.H.,** 'Evaluation of the risk and age of onset of cancer and behavioural disorders in gonadectomised Vizslas' *Journal of the American Veterinary Medical Association* (2014)

❧ Index